Social Drama

BERT AMIES, BERNIE WARREN, ROB WATLING

Social Drama

JOHN CLARE BOOKS
LONDON

First Published John Clare Books, 1986
PO Box 404
106 Cheyne Walk
London SW10 0JR
© Bert Amies, Bernie Warren, Rob Watling

ISBN 0 906549 52 3

Printed and bound in Great Britain by
SRP Ltd., Exeter, Devon

Contents

Foreword

John Tomlinson, Director of Education,
Cheshire

In the forms of ritual, sympathetic magic and tribal memory-maintenance the drama is probably the oldest of the human arts. In every civilization drama in some form or other has played a significant part; at times of high civilization it generally assumes even greater significance in both the sophisticated and the popular mind. In view of this, it is odd how recently drama as a vehicle for education has come to be understood (still less generally accepted) and how fiercely we have to fight for its retention, along with the other arts of mankind, in periods of resignation and retrenchment.

This book is about an even more recently established element of drama in education, which has been given the soubriquet Social Drama. It had its origins in work with individuals and groups largely cut off from society and having little or no opportunity to participate in creative activities. It draws on all the treasure-house of dramatic activities but also strongly calls into action another fundamental source of human development: play. In games, both traditional and invented, it is possible to explore oneself and human relationships in ways which can help to build self-knowledge, self-confidence and greater understanding of other people.

Under the leadership of Bert Amies (whom I have known since my own early days in the administration of adult education in Shropshire), he, Rob Watling and Bernie Warren became a professional team extending Social Drama workshops as a wider and wider audience came to demand them. From their own work with the handicapped and the isolated as well as in the mainstreams of pre-school education, schools, colleges and youth service, came the involvement of other teachers and volunteers – clergy, therapists, social workers, psychologists, students and many others. They therefore started to run training workshops and the movement became well-founded and widespread.

I see these developments having significance in many contemporary contexts which are themselves beginning to interact creatively. Educational work with young children and their parents has rediscovered fundamental ideas about how people grow and learn and has helped to redefine the relationship between professional and client so that each contributes to the work in hand. The essence of community education has developed so that it means not only adults using school facilities out of school hours, but also the education of the pupils – especially the adolescent – being founded in the use by teachers of the human and physical resources of the environment and the capacity of the school to give something back to their community in return. The post-industrial society is beginning to make us think seriously about what life-long education could mean just at the time when three generations of publicly-provided education have produced a generation of adults who want to have more say over their own lives and are willing to form groups to pursue their ends – from civil rights, housing associations, self-help groups, pre-school playgroups, to

Greenpeace and Greenham Common. This could be one of the most creative ages in all educational history – if only policy makers had the vision of the practitioners, both lay and professional.

Until that day dawns, we must each do what we can in our own particular field, and give thanks for the efforts of fellow workers in other parts of the village whose crops and methods can also nourish us. I see Social Drama, and the enthusiasm and insight which informs this book, as part of the current renaissance of thinking about how people learn and develop and an example of the courage and creativity shown in this generation of teachers.

Chester,   John Tomlinson
April, 1984

Preface

This book is the latest result of the work in Social Drama pioneered over the last twenty years by Bert Amies, primarily in schools and colleges in Shropshire. Nearly ten years ago Rob Watling and Bernie Warren joined Bert in his work and as a result Social Drama was extended to a much wider audience. Many of these people were often isolated from society and rarely, if ever, allowed to participate in creative activities for themselves. Slowly the demand for Social Drama workshops grew. The word was out that there was a team of professionals who would travel to hospitals, schools and other institutions to run sessions. The resulting transformations in the behaviour of the children and adults who participated created a curiosity in the professionals who worked with these individuals full-time. As a result there was an increasing demand for us to run training workshops. From this work with such diverse groups as volunteers, clergy, teachers, therapists, social workers, students, and psychologists has come the overwhelming number of requests to put our work 'down on paper'.

Social Drama: Towards a Therapeutic Curriculum is the result of these requests. In it we seek to provide a guide and resource book for teachers, therapists and other professionals working with mentally, physically or emotionally handicapped people as well as for those working in mainstream education or working more informally with groups. We describe how we became involved with and committed to Social Drama; the importance of play and Social Drama's development from its traditional roots; the nature and problems of leadership; the application of Social Drama with a wide range of groups and the overall values of the dramatic process in the social, physical and cognitive education of all people. We hope that we can stimulate professionals into using creative activities with their groups and to this end we have included a selection of games and activities and a guide to further reading in this area.

This book is a testament to the huge strides that Social Drama has taken since we first groped our way through the process of integrating the disparate influences we brought to bear on our work. It is not simply a raconteurs' return through pleasant memories, though throughout the text the reader will find anecdotes that relate to a specific point. What we have tried to do is distil the essence of our way of working, and to relate this to the specific needs of individuals and groups. We have been spurred less by a concern with uniqueness (any reputable professional will admit the universality of dramatic material) than by a concern to persuade people that creativity and innovation can and will flourish, in even the most isolated communities, if only they are given the chance.

I wish to express my sincere gratitude to all the people who have influenced not only my way of working but also my way of being throughout the years. My 'mentors' have come in all shapes and sizes, some have been my teachers whilst others have been my students. In particular I must mention Derek Akers, Bob Whyte, Fred Keating, Dennis Gibbons, Bernie Goddery, Yon, Peter Senior and Alan Robertson, all of whom, in their different ways, have slowly pursued their art forms in a most sensitive and humane manner in spite of pressures from outside to do differently. Their slow and patient approaches are an example for us all.

I must express my sincerest gratitude to my great friends and collaborators Rob and Bert. There is so much that I owe you both, so many fond memories we have shared – I would simply like to say thank you for everything you have done to enrich my life.

I would like to thank Dottie for her continued support for this project. When we first approached her with the idea of this book, nearly 3 years ago, she gave us the good advice that publishing is a slow business which needs a lot of patience. Thank you Dottie for your patience.

To Roberta, my wife and colleague in so much of my work, I must communicate my gratitude. This work has been read by her in all its various stages. Her contributions to my sections and her comments about the others have made this a much more interesting and readable work. Once again I thank you for being who you are and for being the source of my continued inspiration and strength.

This book is dedicated to all those people who were part of the early explorations in Social Drama. The part that each of you had in the development of this work cannot be overestimated. Thank you, one and all, for sharing part of your selves with us. It is to you, and all those groups of people who came after you, that this book really belongs.

B.W.   Kelowna, British Columbia.
                                                    January 1984.

It has fallen to me to fit together the 'patchwork quilt' of our different contributions. I must thank Bert and Bernie for tolerating the way I have interfered with their prose where I have tried to provide us with a more uniform style. Special thanks must go to Alan Watling and Nicky James for their help at the proof-reading stage.

In writing of our own involvement with Social Drama we have all found it useful to write in the first person from time to time. To help the reader identify us we have initialled our different chapter- and section-headings, though we have all co-operated on the final version throughout.

We have tried not to make assumptions about the sex of people involved in Social Drama sessions and have attempted to strike a balance between the use of 'he' and 'she' throughout the text. We hope this leads to equanimity and clarity.

Superior figures in the text refer to notes at the end of each chapter. Suggested reading is arranged under chapter headings in the Bibliography.

R.W.   Wrexham, Clwyd.
January 1984.

Introduction

A therapeutic curriculum sounds much more positive than an academic curriculum, and indeed there has long been a need for one. Fortunately a majority of people manage to adjust their lives successfully after even the most formal of educations, but this is because they have enough natural flexibility to do so and not because their educational experience has helped them in any way. The result of this has been that successive administrations have believed that they have got education 'right'. That it is not yet 'right' is plainly obvious to many of us, although it does seem to be marginally better than it was. If we contrast what we know of young unemployed people in the Great Depression of the 1920's with today's young unemployed we find that there is a shade less despair around, and this could be because education since 1945 has helped produce young people who have pride and independence. But the signs are not all good, and there arc now some people in positions of power who wish to turn education back to the paucity of pre-1939 days.

It is on good educational practice that we can build therapeutic innovations for all and thus enhance and consolidate the more formal educational necessities. We hear of the profiling approach to education – something which has not come before time. This method would remove the tyranny of final examinations and take into account some of the actual *developments* of the student. The progress of all students would be monitored throughout their schooling: it is the *journey* and not the *destination* that is important in education. Contributions which students can make outside the framework of their school curriculum would be noted and rewarded and some of the real achievements in life would not continue to go unrecognized.

A profiling method of education would do well to depend very heavily on something rather like Social Drama, where students could make contacts, experiment with ideas, and then develop them through interaction. We know of no better place for assessing and developing the potential of any person than the natural, happy, unconfined atmosphere of the Social Drama workshop. It is here, through games, improvisation, experiment and discussion that knowledge already acquired through formal and informal learning can be opened out. In fact all the human faculties can be exercised here, which is why it is successful with so many different groups.

Therapy is usually used in the sense of something being curative, but it can also be used to describe those things which help us to achieve and maintain our peak condition. That Social Drama is a form of therapy cannot be denied. It can be used to cure when a cure is needed, to open out a closed personality or to enhance personal development. There is no age, class or ability barrier to it.

B.A.   Longnor, Shropshire.
                                                   January 1984.

SECTION I
THE ROAD TO SOCIAL DRAMA

1. The Beginnings of Social Drama

The term Social Drama was first coined in the early 1960's. Its evolution has been a long and complicated affair (it is still changing) and its importance to us is covered by the following accounts of our own involvement in Social Drama workshops. They outline our similar convictions and slightly different approaches as well as our specific interests.

BERT AMIES

I often think that Social Drama was waiting for me to find it.

As a young boy I was an avid player of group games indoors, outdoors and in the school playground. Until the age of eight I did not have many playmates at home because we lived on a fairly isolated farm, but there was my brother, my sister and the teenage girl who lived in to help my mother. Occasionally a cousin came to stay with us for several weeks, and the son of one of the farm workers would show up from time to time. In summer we boys would play out in the orchard, the fields, or the farm buildings; in winter we played in either the kitchen or back kitchen. The summer games were often connected with farm themes so that we were birds, pigs or horses, but we also played at houses and ships. On winter evenings we played board games such as Snakes and Ladders or simple card games, but sometimes there would be enough of us to play some of the traditional party games such as I Spy, Hunt the Slipper, Spinning the Platter and others of that kind. My brother, my cousin and I also continued to play our creative farm games indoors. At school there were enough children to make up groups for quite elaborate games, and whilst I was there playground singing games were still popular with the younger children. We played all the seasonal games: marbles, skipping, skimming fag cards, Jack o' Five Stones, conkers, hoops and Hop Scotch. There were also games in the playground which did not involve singing, such as, Sheep, Sheep, Come Over, (see game 7) and Grandmother's Footsteps (see game 33). The senior boys and girls played some team games out in my father's field but I never got caught up in this. I watched cricket because my father and uncles were keen players, but I never wanted to play. We sometimes played a kind of half-hearted football but we did not obey any of the rules because we did not know any. My father hopefully bought my brother and I a cricket bat, but all we played with that was French Cricket. We sometimes played Rounders if enough children came but more often we played the simpler version known as Puss in the Corner. Hide and Seek was always a popular game.

I particularly enjoyed Christmas and birthday parties, where there were enough people to engage in some of the more elaborate indoor games. Many of these games have stood the test of time and are still used at Social Drama sessions. At the age of eight my family moved to a farm nearer Birmingham. It was in a populous area where there were many other children to play with. My games–playing patterns continued right up until I went to a minor Public School at the age of eleven. Even there it was possible to avoid the competitive team games, and to continue to play creative games in the lunch hour.

As I grew older my games took the form of putting on plays and pantomimes with local playmates, but I was still particularly hooked on party games, and I was always overjoyed when my mother said we could have a party. I would spend days planning games for the event, some games were to be old favourites and others I invented. The new ones did not always work, but I became better and better at devising them.

Later on I produced plays in the village hall, with a youth club, and something of a climax was reached with the 'end of show' parties which went on into the small hours. I realized what a strong bonding these party games were capable of creating. The youth club began to put on social evenings and I took the organizing role more and more; there was some dancing but the evening was mostly spent in games-playing.

After drama and music training I took up teaching. I taught creative drama to secondary boys, and then to mixed classes in a junior school, but it did not occur to me to introduce drama games as they had played no part in my own training. At school parties I was back 'on form' again with games. I was also directing several adult drama groups who seemed very willing to hold after show parties. Yes, you've guessed, a great many party games were played but I still did not see the actual link with drama.

I was appointed as a County Drama and Arts Adviser in 1958. I had to do a great deal of work in schools, with adult drama groups, and to organize drama courses for teachers and youth club members. On the courses, I was teaching drama techniques, movement and voice production, and I seemed to keep everybody happy, but I began to feel that I had got into a rut. Then in the 60's I became aware that a new approach to drama was afoot. It was brought home to me by the many personalities

I was inviting to lecture and demonstrate on courses at Att-
ingham Park Adult College. The visitors included practitioners
from the theatre and from drama-in-education. It became
obvious that there was much more to drama than mere theatre
skills, there was also the motivational force which could unlock
the acting drive which lies dormant in many people. I realized
that it was one thing to train students who wish to enter the
theatrical profession, or at the very least to be successful in an
amateur drama group, but quite another to encourage pleasure
and self-discovery in those who have no such ambition. Fur-
thermore such Social Drama work done for the enlightenment
of the latter can have value for the former. Motivation was the
key and this never failed to work when party games and drama
games provided the stimulus. It became clear that each game
had a 'pay off' (i.e. apart from the dynamics of the game there
were developments in life skills which included voice, movement, interaction and even characterization). This was an
exciting discovery because it widened the range of people who
were likely to benefit from drama work. Peter Slade had seen
the value of creative drama for all children, now I had found a
form of creative drama for adolescents and adults. It was a short
step to the realization that the human condition is one of role-
playing and that under the right circumstances all people are
happy to play. Social Drama began to feature as an element in
my drama courses and the number of people wishing to attend
increased.

At about this time I was conducting one drama session a week
at the local Art School. The students had taken very readily to
drama although only two of them had any interest in going into
the theatre to work. They were all studying drama as part of a
widely based arts curriculum. They were happy to study music
and movement, improvisations, play reading and rehearsal,

verse speaking and even play writing, but when I introduced structured games-playing the whole work took on a new meaning; their natural dramatic nature surfaced so that practical creativity took the place of the academic learning. I was joined by another member of Staff from the local Technical College and regular Wednesday afternoon sessions of Social Drama were set up as a choice subject for students from all the local further education colleges. As I and other members of Staff grew in confidence and became convinced of the value of what we were doing, so the bonding of the group, and the unleashing of their contribution strengthened. We moved into my studio/ rehearsal room which became a revered meeting place. More students began to appear and they asked if they could bring along other friends who found themselves at a loose end. At times the problem became one of sheer weight of numbers. We leaders began to encourage the students to take leadership and we were not disappointed. They invented games, tried simulations, improvised plays and most important of all they began to expect or lead discussions on a wide range of subjects which concerned them. They seemed to have found a perfect medium for vital communication. As time went on, and especially in the summer months, they would go out into the town with some specific objective. They came back to discuss what they had observed, how people behave in shops, on the pavement, in the library etc. and they did indeed discover that 'The proper study of mankind is man'. What they were doing and discovering became a talking point in their colleges and there was an eager group of new students waiting to join at the beginning of each year. Students were expected to change their option groups each term but for the social drama work to have any benefit I insisted that it must be conducted over at least a year. Many students stayed on for a second year. What was done and what can be achieved is outlined elsewhere in this book. I like to say that social drama is a kind of therapy for the normal with the proviso that it is difficult to define what is normal. Certainly the Social Drama group has often included people who were at some kind of risk and they gained benefit from being accepted into a caring group. Even the most unhappy and withdrawn person seems to blossom in the environment of Social Drama and it has been one of the great pleasures of my life to see some such people awakened and made trustful. My own involvement with Social Drama has also led to new developments in my work as a director with amateur drama groups. For my part I count myself fortunate that through all this work I have gained more understanding of people of all ages, and I am grateful that so many students have put their trust in me.

BERNIE WARREN

In 1975 I had come to a major crossroad in my life. Until this time I had always wanted to be a doctor and to this end I had just completed two years of a Bachelor of Science degree in Human Biology. I was, however, extremely unhappy in my course of studies and was spending most of my time on extra-mural activities. In particular I was performing as a musician/actor with a travelling Theatre Company and being involved in local community action groups. I had made up my mind to take at least a year out from my studies and had accepted a summer job working with Protestant and Catholic children from Northern Ireland, children who had been severely disturbed by the 'civil war'. The future after that summer was extremely uncertain. Blind chance and a job in community work took me to Shrewsbury.

Shrewsbury is the last of the English Shire towns and is not noted for its role in changing the shape of world history. In fact to many Shrewsbury is a sleepy backwater, a hot-bed of rural conservatism, barely crawling its way into the second half of the twentieth century. Yet beneath this sleepy exterior with its inertia and general distrust of foreigners (i.e. all people not born and bred in the county) there is a basic down-to-earth honesty and a willingness, once the imagination is engaged, to become actively involved. This involvement is not on a superficial level, as I have found to be the case in large urban cities with transient populations, but is on a deeply committed personal level, one that implicitly acknowledges the value of other human beings. What I found in Shrewsbury was an underlying care and concern for the less fortunate members of the community. This concern and to an extent the area's inherent conservatism were strong catalysts in the development of our work in Social Drama and subsequently in our collaboration on this book.

It was in 1975 that I first met Bert Amies and Rob Watling. Rob and I were employed by the Community Council of Shropshire as Community Catalysts. Our job was to be stimulators of community involvement by the young people of the county. We shared an office, a bicycle, a moped, a flat (all of which came with the job) and a sense of humour and righteous indignation – which were our 'trade marks'. We met Bert Amies, then County Drama and Arts Adviser, through Bill Morris, a member of the advisory board supervising our work. Bill was a sociology teacher at the local college and the coordinator of the Wednesday afternoon liberal studies options. For nearly ten years Bill and Bert had been running a Social Drama session for local college and art school students. Rob and I helped to expand the range of activities which made up the afternoon sessions but we were also able to see the implications and benefits of 'exporting' the sessions to a wider audience. To this extent we actively sought to bring the Social Drama programme into the lives of school children, senior citizens, mentally handicapped people and many other groups throughout the county. As time went by our 'sphere of influence' increased with many requests coming from all corners of the British Isles for us to run Social Drama training sessions. However, in those first two years (1975–76) Bert, Rob, myself and occasionally Bill visited any and every school, hospital, group home, club or other institution in Shropshire who would have us come and run a session of Social Drama.

The substance of our work in Social Drama is to a large extent a product of our own backgrounds, interest and personalities. However, it goes without saying that our work has been influenced by those innovators who preceded us and those who are our contemporaries working in such diverse fields as Psychology, Psychotherapy, Educational Drama, Role Theory, Actor Training, Human Communications and the Creative Arts Therapies. In addition to this influence (by such notables as Berne, Brook, Freud, Goffman, Jung, Moreno, Maslow, Perls, Slade, Spolin and Stanislavski), we have been strongly affected, in our development of Social Drama, by the centuries of Dramatic Literature with all the rich insight that it brings to human interactions and to the human condition.

The beginnings of Social Drama were in a love for people and a belief in the therapeutic power of the dramatic process. More than this there was a friendship and camaraderie that grew out of the work. Our skills and philosophies differed but between us we had a bond which enabled us to work together. Leadership was rarely, if ever, discussed. The roles of leaders and assistants were dictated by the needs of the group and the moment. This was an essential component in the development of what became

Social Drama. It was only through this unspoken give-and-take, this empathy, that we were able to develop the philosophy, methods and material.

My primary interest in Shropshire was in Social Drama and its value to young people within the community. Since those early days I have spread my wings. What started for me as a means of engaging a larger audience with the concept of community action became a relaxation, an adventure in human development and a life-long challenge: the challenge of allowing all people access to their own creative potential. I am no longer exclusively concerned with Social Drama, although the philosophies and techniques of those earlier days can be clearly seen, imprinted indelibly on my current way of working.

My work over the last five years has taken me more and more into the realm of drama/theatre for, by and with special populations, and into the more treacherous area of Arts Therapy. I have recently been teaching courses at the University of Calgary related to Drama and Dance-Movement Therapy. I work as a consultant arts therapist with hospitals, school boards and group homes and as a practising arts therapist with various groups of mentally or physically handicapped people. I have just completed my term as the first President of the Alberta Arts Therapy Association, and edited a book on the uses of the creative arts in therapy.[1] Yet despite this move to a different continent and to a more specialized area of work, the memories, experiences and enjoyment gained through my initial work in Social Drama will not only stay with me throughout my life, they will continue to be the cornerstone in my approach to the people I work with. The beginnings for me were in being a part of Social Drama. In writing this book I hope that it will be a beginning for some of you.

ROB WATLING

In the Autumn of 1975 I went with Bernie Warren to my first Social Drama workshop. In a dusty room full of people, stage props and theatre memories I found myself playing games with enthusiasm and enjoyment – a sensation I had not experienced for years. At school 'Games' had been equated in my mind with abject misery – the ritual torture and humiliation of the inept by big-booted experts (especially the staff). In this room, however, people were playing games without scoring points off each other. They were playing for their own sakes and for every one else's. Sharing, not winning. Giving, not losing. This was the invigorating sort of play I could remember from my youth.

I don't recall ever missing a Wednesday afternoon Social Drama session all the time I was in Shrewsbury. What happened in the rehearsal room seemed so relevant to what went on outside, particularly Bernie's and my work as Community Catalysts. Before long we started taking on more active roles in the sessions (one of the 'rules' of Social Drama is that eventually anyone can contribute to the leadership). I never decided to do it, but was so simply at home with what was happening that I wanted to give as part of my sharing. It appears that Bernie and I stumbled in on Bert Amies and his work just at the right time – when it was full of latent power and needing to expand. We were working with all sorts of groups in the community and, almost without thinking, started to use Social Drama throughout the week. We used it first as a regular component of our work in a local psychiatric hospital, then with the physically handicapped, the elderly, the young, the disadvantaged, the ill and the 'normal'. It worked every time and we became as famous for our 'silly games' as for our more orthodox community work. Underneath it all, though, I already knew that these were not just silly games. I knew that I played them seriously and that I expected others to play them seriously too. I knew that underneath our flippancy and good humour we were dealing with material that could help make the difference between successful and unsuccessful lives. I couldn't explain it to people but said that they had better come and experience it for themselves.

I left Shropshire in 1976 and went to Stirling University to study English and Folklore. It didn't seem likely that my interest in Social Drama would be sustained, but I was soon prominent in the University Dramatic Society and used games and exercises to train students as actors. They helped develop voice, movement and characterization and in the formation of a cohesive cast. It was not until later that I came across the splendid work of Clive Barker in this area.

On leaving University I realized that my ambitions did not lie in the conventional theatre, as I had begun to think. I teamed up with three friends to form a revue company for the summer and I enjoyed the writing, the rehearsals, the performances, even the penury to a certain extent. But I wanted more. I wanted to work *with* people, rather than *for* them or *at* them. So I packed my bags and headed for Wales and a job in a therapeutic community for adolescents. My brief was to design, develop and maintain a programme of drama- and video-based activities. I was given an empty hall, some impressive video gear, a telephone and the emotional, educational and behavioural difficulties of 200 youngsters. I needed a lifeline and, surprise, surprise, it turned out to be Social Drama. The youngsters enjoyed it, and it seemed the ideal way of helping them to develop as individuals and as members of an increasingly demanding society.

Two years later, as I started to build up my own freelance work, it became essential to put Social Drama into a broader theoretical framework. I started to read more about psychology and alternative therapies, to learn about the problems of applying group techniques to physical, mental and social handicaps. But in particular (in preparation for a tour of North America in 1982) I started to draw links between what I now knew and felt about Social Drama and the study of Folklore I had made in Stirling. I had adopted games playing out of practical convictions rather than theoretical ones, and I knew that traditional societies selected and developed their own systems in similar ways. I had long realised that many of the games and exercises of Social Drama were traditional material, created, changed, passed on and revived over hundreds of years. I also knew that groups invented new games in very traditional ways. I began to explain certain aspects of my work with direct references to folklore and it is still a developing interest.

As I move on now into new areas of community work I still consider myself to be a catalyst in my employment, my leisure and my involvement with issues like the peace movement. In a more complex, more demanding and more dangerous world individuals and communities need continually to learn, to develop and to celebrate. Social Drama is a perfect medium for all three.

Notes

1 B. Warren, ed., *Using the Creative Arts in Therapy* (London: Croom Helm, 1984).

2. The Importance of Play and Games
(B.A. & R.W.)

Play is a particular type of behaviour displayed by all mammals. We can identify it in puppies, lion cubs, lambs, baby chimpanzees and many other young animals. In some species (including man) play remains an element of behaviour into adulthood, and it is apparent that the further we look up the evolutionary scale the more play we come across. It is a particularly important element in social grouping, especially for humans.

It was at the turn of the last century that Karl Groos, Professor of Philosophy at the University of Basle began to take play seriously as an academic subject and to regard it as functional.[1] He had noticed that play was most prevalent in the higher orders and suggested that it was a vital element in helping these animals combat the more complicated demands of their development. Animals do not play because they are young, he suggested, but they have their youth because they must play. Groos believed that play was essentially practice at life skills, which helped develop all sorts of instinctive animal behaviour (basic and complex movement, catching prey, escaping from enemies, courtship, etc). He suggested that when species like the primates needed to develop more complicated life skills they indulged in greater amounts of playful practice, and he identified teasing and love-play as two of the significant examples of functional play in humans, pointing out that there were psychological benefits to be gained from pleasurable experiences. Groos helped to lend respectability to the play-research that has been carried out since – particularly the vast amounts that have been done in the second half of this century. It is not our intention to review this research or even to refer to it extensively. We readily acknowledge Social Drama's eclecticism and offer our own analysis of purposeful play as we have experienced it ourselves and used it in our workshops.

Before we examine the importance and functions of play and games it is worth stressing the concept, put so succintly by the Opies, that 'play is unrestricted, games have rules'.[2] Human games differ from all other animal play in that they are guided by pre-arranged, collectively-determined rules. They involve volition, and thus exercise the will, which would appear to be a uniquely human capacity. If we combine this with Groos's theory that play helps us to develop vital life skills and to experience necessary pleasures, we can begin to understand the role that Social Drama with its emphasis on enjoyable, social, experimental play can have in helping people to achieve their full potential.

THE IMPORTANCE OF PLAY TO CHILDREN (B.A.)

The most common question asked by children of other children, or even of adults, is probably, 'Will you play with me?' It is very easy, but wrong, for adults to assume that they invented play to keep children occupied. Play is a way of life for children, Nature's way. It is part of the process of growing up.

For the good of our race we should reflect seriously on the nature of play. True creative play is a learning process which is likely to be successful because it is so enjoyable that children become completely absorbed in it. In the late 40's and early 50's an educational movement known as 'The play way of learning' was developed. It was well understood and welcomed by many teachers but completely misunderstood and mishandled by others. Whilst traces of it remain it has, for the most part, disappeared into the past. The reasoning behind the movement was sound, seeking as it did to bridge the gap between the child and adult world, but to do this successfully teachers needed to recall and accept their own childhood. Many people find this extremely difficult to do until they reach old age. The rapport between children and the elderly is often remarked upon. I have conducted many courses with teachers where at some point I have encouraged a 'group telling' of childhood anecdotes. One favourite method is to ask each teacher in turn to describe his childhood den. It is very heartening to see faces light up and to realize that this is something which most adults have given no thought to since they left school. For the teacher to try to contact the child from his mature role pattern can often be disastrous even when the role is one as of parent to child. Most people are familiar with the biblical quotation 'When I was a child, I spake as a child, I understood as a child, I thought as a child: but when I became a man, I put away childish things.' These words have often troubled me because they seem to dismiss childhood as a lesser state and they imply that the child in us can be abandoned. I feel that there is an inherent danger in taking the words too literally because although we need to reflect upon our adult persona we also need to accept the child who is still at the core of our being. Some childish attitudes should be modified but in the case of the artist (and surely we are all that) we must retain that part of the child which feeds us with a genuine sense of wonder. Putting away our childhood is repressing an important part of ourselves – one which we should always be able to face up to for good or ill.

There are many divisions and sub-divisions in children's play but there are two which are easily identifiable. These are solo play, and group play. Both serve a very important function in child development. When a small child plays alone she will often build up an imaginary world around herself, and as she loses herself in her fantasy she will verbalize with great seriousness and even sing and dance. It is a great privilege to watch children thus engaged. At such times the onlooker should never be intrusive. What one first notices is that the child has gone into a world of her own making. What she is doing is not naïve or precocious and it does not warrant titters of laughter from an audience. If the child becomes over-aware that her play is being observed her behaviour can become self-indulgent. There are times when an adult speaks to a child at play only to find that the child does not appear to hear. The child is, in fact, being no more unco-operative than an adult who has become preoccupied with some problem and who is temporarily out of reach of his companions. For this reason it is not always wise for a teacher to ask a child to stop daydreaming and to come back to the matter in hand. The matter in hand may not actually be as important to the child, at that time, as her own thoughts. The crux of this fairly common problem of trying to gain the child's attention lies in the fact that the teacher can feel ignored, less important and, therefore, challenged in a situation where he believes he should be in total control. Here is a case where the teacher should remember his own childhood and his own periods of meditation.

Most parents realize that their young children can become totally involved in play; the only cause for worry is when this is *not* the case. They also know that it can be very difficult to catch the attention of the playing child even if they want her to do something as practical as to get ready for a meal. As far as the child is concerned the make-believe world has become the real one and what is happening in that world is of vital importance. That is not to say that the adult should never intrude; there are times when it is essential and in this case the child begins to learn the rules of the adult world which she must one day inhabit.

In their make-believe world some children adopt an organizing role and it is possible that they are putting in a bid for leadership. I know of one boy, just approaching his fourth birthday, who is quite happy to play with adults when there are no other children around. He escorted two friends and myself, all of us past our prime, out into the garden to a low shed under a yew tree. He intended to have an entertainment; in this case a circus. He was the ring-master and we, two men and a woman, were in turn lions and tigers, a fat woman, two tall men, dwarfs, and then 'Tree Cows'. The latter puzzled me until I realized that there were cattle in the field next to the garden and that they often came under the other side of the yew tree for shade. They had obviously caught Tommy's imagination but the problem was that he wanted his tree cows to get on the shed roof and climb up the tree. We tried to oblige. He announced each of his circus items in grand style – he had taken the role of Superman – and we had to perform. The performance was rather a long one and it had to include some singing (his father is a singer and entertainer). When the game came to an end, or to be more precise when we adults were flagging, he was unwilling to let the show come to an end. He tried various ruses to keep us going. Finally I was left alone with him whereupon he tried to hold me to play by turning into a shopkeeper who was trying to sell me pieces of bark from some logs. I found it necessary to terminate the game and only did so by the rather cowardly trick of suggesting that if he came into the house he could have some orange juice.

A few days after this episode I conducted a drama session at a residential course for disabled children. After a few drama games the group settled into a play improvisation and a young girl took charge of the proceedings. She was confined to a wheel chair. All adults who were helping with the course, with one exception, were soon inserted into the play. The exception was a woman helper who said that she could never involve herself in creative play. I gave myself the function of improvising at the piano to develop the atmosphere and story line but in that I was mistaken. A point came in the story/play when a flying green dragon was needed and the young organizer cast me without hesitation. It was then that I realized that I was as involved in the story as the children were. The play ended with a wedding. It was clear to me that although these children were severely disabled they had healthy expectations of a normal life. During the course of the play an eight-year-old girl had not been well and she lay on one of the reclining beds while the others performed. As the play drew to its close someone said that the wicked witch had turned into a beautiful princess. By common consent the group decided that the girl who was unwell was the princess. She was at once ready to join in and she is the one who was married, to live happily ever after.

There are very real values for children playing in this way. Each child is using the opportunity to experiment with their own individuality and can learn how they are being received by others. It is often difficult to teach adolescents or adults the rules of interpersonal relationships, but children discover and absorb them through their games. Animal play is practice at tasks that will one day have to be faced for real. When children play they, too, are rehearsing for their adult life. They will cope with the adult world best if they have already adjusted to other people through play.

A difficult point can be reached in children's group play, or improvisations, when there are too many cowboys and not enough Indians. Several children get carried away in their imagination and put in a bid for leadership. In this case the principle game or activity can get split up into several sub-plots. This often happens even when the whole group has decided on a particular story-line from the outset. It is quite normal where children are in control of the proceedings. If an adult intrudes too much this may not happen and the creativity is likely to be in a lower key. The emergence of sub-plots is to be welcomed as a significant contribution to the learning process. More children have a real function; after all they are not working on a play in the adult sense where a finished production will be shown to an audience. If they have got a finished production in mind they have moved out of the realm of genuine, creative, child drama, in which they should quite naturally be experimenting with vital skills such as language, movement, body language, role-playing and the development of values.

Language is used in two distinct ways in improvised play. There is the contractual language which is used to decide on a play theme and to outline how it will develop, and to be used 'sotto voce' to give further instructions during the course of the play, and there is the artistic language of the characters them-selves. The first is as important as the second and it should not be interrupted by too much adult advice. As children get older their work will move more into the direction of the adult concept of a play.

It has always been realised that children's active play is likely to have a physical pay-off. As children play they move rhythmi-cally and naturally, and their bodies can develop through running, climbing and jumping, not to mention crawling and squirming. There is a limitation of this in severely handicapped children but such active play as can be managed should be encouraged. Rhythmical movèment stimulates rhythmical speaking, and even thinking, so it is here that play begins to build the rounded personality. The unity of physical skill and grace coupled with artistic awareness was well understood in ancient Greece. Perhaps the time is long overdue for reintroducing music skill and poetry writing and speaking into the Olympic Games.

There is also another language children have to master if they are going to be successful in society and it is a language which is not generally taught. It is body language, a language of physical signs. For most people a familiarity with this language starts in childhood and we go on reading it for the rest of our lives. We do not always use words to betray how we feel, or we might not find the correct words to express our feelings; the language of gesture, touch, eye contact, physical stance or attitude, characterization etc. will express things more exactly. Handicapped children often depend upon body language for communication, particularly the totally deaf.

Role-playing behaviour is learnt by each individual through observation and life experience, and the groundwork for it is laid in children's play. There are those who deny the whole concept of the role-playing nature of man. Usually they have not recognized the subtle shifts of role which take place according to the situation they find themselves in. It should be obvious, for example that one's behaviour on a beach is very different from behaviour in a place of worship, and that the office persona is unlike the person relaxing at home. Perhaps the concept would be more acceptable if we spoke of varying facets rather than varying roles. Facets of our personality shift slightly according to whom we are with, and it is important that children become skilled in this adaptability. Creative play helps them to do just this.

The only deliberate teaching of body language or role-playing is done with acting students in drama academies because such knowledge will form the central core of their stage work. For the rest of us it is acquired knowledge which starts in childhood through contacts in games. The trouble is that some of us get the language or the rules wrong and in extreme cases can become social misfits. Yet again there are others who understand the rules but deliberately break them. Some role-playing becomes so anti-social that the services of a psychiatrist have to be called upon to try to unravel the chaos which is causing deep distress. Most of us want to be liked and accepted but there are those who seem to spend most of their time making others feel distressed. They are often the victims of unsuccessful childhoods or have been confused by parental control. Children who play successfully and adjust to each other in a civilized way stand a better chance of becoming well adjusted adults but there has to be a partnership between children and adults right from the start. We have the awful example of children deprived of an adult presence in William Golding's *Lord of the Flies*. Children will experiment with cruelty as well as compassion in their games.

Through games children learn what is good and acceptable, and what aspects of behaviour society frowns upon. They are bound to learn naughty things, especially in the sexual field; fortunately most of us did not miss out on that. The whole area of sexual education is a morass in Great Britain; in other countries, Holland for example, they handle the subject with a little less prejudice. Most early sexual knowledge is passed on from child to child and very few of us reach adulthood in total innocence. In the few cases where this does happen it can often be traced back to over-protective parents or a lack of playmates in early years. In a group children learn what words and concepts can be publicly accepted. When, in play, a child says or does something shocking, the group reaction can vary from embarrassed titters to gasps of horror. If an adult is present on this charged occasion the children will at once look to see how he has coped with the outrage.

The first structured game played by most children is usually 'Peep-bo' and even in this simple exercise we can see them experimenting with one of the problems of growing up. They are practising separation – taking themselves out of their parents' sight for a brief moment and exploring the sensations that this stimulates in themselves and the adults. This sort of play develops through many different stages into the traditional children's games like the street singing game. These have an underlying, and quite unspoken psychological force which make them a necessary part of understanding the world into which the children are growing. Many of the games have a socializing effect, building group-bonding and confidence in a hostile and challenging world. Conformity with the games' structures allows the child to be accepted in the group and ritual gives the feeling of invoking magic forces or the gods. In some of the games there is a triumphant victory over the adversities that the children are beginning to learn about. We can see this clearly in games like Ring-a-ring o' roses, which is said to date from the time of the plague of London. The symptoms of the plague, and one of the antidotes are poetically reviewed in the game, and then the inevitable death happens. It does not take much imagination to understand how children of the time feared the plague, and death. They could play out this ritual, and still be gloriously alive at the end of it. Another chanting game, We are the Roman Soldiers, deals with death and mutilation. The players lose one arm, then another, then eyes and legs, and then they are 'Dead and in the grave', but there is the triumphant final verse, 'Now we're up and 'live again.'

The Farmer's in His Den, is probably one of the oldest games. It would not be unreasonable to guess that it was based on adult rituals which children saw being enacted; in this case fertility rituals which were common-place in early times. The key to this game lies in the final chant, and because in the latter part of this century that chant has fallen into disuse, the meaning of the game has become more obscure. When children played the game in my youth there were local variations in the words of the chants, but the general structure of the thing remained constant. The game started with one child, the farmer, in the middle, and all the other children joined hands round him. They began to sing, 'The farmer's in his den, The farmer's in his den, Hi ay tiddley ay, The farmer's in his den.' The next verse stated that the farmer wanted a wife, whereupon one was chosen by the farmer, and she joined him in the circle. The game continued with the wife wanting a child, the child wanting a dog, and the dog wanting a bone. Nowadays the game tends to end with all chanting 'We all pat the bone' etc., but the game used to end with the whole group bouncing the unfortunate bone up and down, chanting 'The bone won't stand' etc., and at the end the child representing the bone was thrown by the combined force of the group, across the playground. I well remember playing this complete version, and I seem to remember that unpopular children were picked for the bone. You can either choose to see this game as nonsensical, country children's one, or you can see in it the historical remnant of a fertility ceremony. If you should think that the latter idea is far-fetched, just reflect upon fertility gods whose effigies are engraved in chalk turf on the South Downs and elsewhere. They were there for all, including the children, to see. The monks, in the Middle Ages, censored these effigies by filling in all the naughty bits, but there is still one left at Cerne Abbas, in Dorset, where the fertility motif survives, intact.

These children's games, then, are strongly ritualistic. They are also repetitive, and we shall look at the dangers of children returning repeatedly to the same theme in chapter 4, but the street games are recitals, not adventures in creativity. I have hinted that the traditional singing games are probably imitations of adult behaviours which children have witnessed, but after that the games become a pure invention. They are played for enjoyment and their repeated forms give them a sense of orderliness and structure – two things which children love to achieve in their creative play. They will soon lose interest in a drama improvisation if either of these factors is missing. Modern children still have a need for ritualistic behaviour and they are always busy creating it.

When older children go out to play some of them will abandon creative activity and turn to bouts of aggressive behaviour. The problem knows no class barriers, it is as likely to occur with children of the wealthy as well as those from deprived homes. It is particularly common with children who have identified themselves as a definite gang. The question of dare comes up and it is then that windows of abandoned houses get broken and other damage occurs to private and public property. This aggressive behaviour has always been with us, indeed it remains with some of us throughout our lives but we find ways of disguising it or practising it in ways which are socially acceptable. In childhood it tends to be bound up with role experiments and in the bid for admiration or leadership of the peer group. As Eric Berne has pointed out,[3] the catching and punishing of young offenders is regarded by them as all part of the 'game'. One solution for these problem children is to turn the power of their aggressive drive towards constructive activity; it must be done so that the constructive alternative becomes more attractive than the destructive one. Some people are working in this field which requires time, patience and money. It is lack of money which prevents many such schemes getting started. I understand that Sweden has successfully tackled this problem over many years past.

So far I have talked about those children who can play quite naturally but some thought must be given to those who have been deprived of play. The deprivation can be due to several causes. There might have been no other children to play with in the area or the child might be a natural loner with whom no one else wants to play: some children are bad mixers. Then there is the case where over-protective parents never allow their child out of doors to play with others. One obvious example of play deprivation can be a child who is handicapped and people in charge of such a child must make themselves aware of the danger and make a point of encouraging play, however limited. These children may become prime candidates for Social Drama and their particular needs are discussed in more detail in Chapter 4.

In the course of my work I have questioned many people about their early play activities and it does not require too great a depth of psychological knowledge to reach conclusions about how play, or the lack of it, has moulded the adults concerned. I have made a point of having some private discussion with adults who are suffering from stress, or distress, or who admit that they are not really coping successfully with life. To give concrete examples here would be betraying a trust but generally speaking those who confess that they were deprived of play are aware that it has affected their life style. One solution is to give them an opportunity to make a very late start by engaging in Social Drama or creative drama. This can give them a chance to begin to experiment with (and understand) unlearned, unwritten rules of role-playing in life.

Some adults have carried a genuine playing drive over into their adult lives. One senses that they are well adjusted and enquiries about early play are generally met with the enthusiastic response that they had a wonderful childhood. In some professions it is essential that the playing drive has been developed. I am thinking of the poet, artist or actor in this respect, but any profession which requires an out-going person, who must be able to relate to others, will attract those who became well adjusted through early child learning. Cold and tense people are often hurt, defensive people and their personality problems often started at a very early age.

It might be argued that professional games players should also have had a full ration of creative play as children but their work could be seen as exactly opposite to this. What they do has to be fiercely competitive and they have often absorbed this from a school system which lays too great a stress on competition. I do not mean that life can be totally divorced from some competitive drive but surely the best competition is self-competition. In the splendid novel *Birdy* by William Wharton, one of the characters says, 'Games are something we've made up to help us forget we've forgotten how to play. Playing is doing something for itself.'

When we think of children playing we think of toys, and the vast toy departments in shops demonstrate their universal appeal. They are a material possession for a very definite child need; children of all cultures have them. Anthropologists and explorers have commented on the fact that even the children of the most remote tribes play with human and animal effigies. Dolls and effigies have been found in excavations of the most ancient sites known to man. The basic toys were always related to life and living things which gave children a chance to understand what they were aspiring to in adult life. Some toys were very inventive as, for example, Peter Brook points out in his book *The Empty Space*. In southern Mexico the adults made toys for their children which probably excited the children as much as a computer game does today. They made little trucks with roller wheels, and this was before it occurred to the adults to apply the same principle of the wheel to the transport of their own heavy goods.[4] The basic doll or cuddly toy is still obviously popular today and it fills a need which the most sophisticated computer game cannot do. Very few children take their computer to bed, but quite a few adults still take their teddy bears. The doll has become the Cindy Doll, and for boys someone provided Action Man: the effigy is still wanted. Many modern toys puzzle the brain and are even meant to educate but the really important ones are those which can give human comfort. Toy manufacturing is big business and marketing forces exert great pressure to convince children that they want expensive and elaborate toys. If the trend continues, coupled with the trend to put children in copies of adult clothes, we shall be returning to the state of affairs of Victorian times when children were thought to be adult at the age of ten, and their needs were regarded as troublesome. Fortunately we are still at the stage where when Mary is puzzling her brain with some educational toy there will be a tap on the door and Susan will be there asking, 'Are you coming out to play?' Then the real learning can begin.

GAMES IN TRADITION (R. W.)

The more we examine children's play the more importance we attach to encouraging healthy creative play among the young. But it is too easy to assume that play is only functional while we are children and that adult play is competitive or 'only for fun'. This common assumption contains two errors: the beliefs that personal development is completed before we enter adulthood; and that fun is not functional. We shall be looking at the role of fun shortly, but before that it is essential to point out that we believe everyone can benefit from games-playing, creativity and the continual exploration of life's components. Social Drama can be used in a remedial setting, but it is not *just* treatment – as we shall constantly stress in this book. It is also an opportunity for recreation, growth and further discovery. Even the most developed garden needs tending and weeding.

Experience convinces us that play is a natural and beneficial activity. My study of folklore convinces me that games (the material of structured human play like Social Drama) are subject to the 'laws' of traditional material. They are a part of our culture which is handed down by word of mouth and by practice from generation to generation, changing and being changed as they go. As such they are best discussed with reference to their social context and their function.[5] This is true for all traditional material: a folk tale is best understood if we know who tells it to whom, where, when, how and why; a traditional game is best understood if we know who plays it, with whom, in what setting, in which season, and so on.

Traditional societies are not wasteful. What they have, they need. This is true not just for their material possessions but for their beliefs, their customs, their songs, their dances, their wise sayings . . . and their games. The folk simply do not persist with anything in their culture which is useless. They will either alter it so that it remains useful or they will discard it. Farm implements, for example, changed hardly at all for centuries until the machine age began. Tools were then redesigned or made obsolete as farming methods changed. The same is true of the artefacts in the kitchen. No one has yet come up with a serious challenge to the wooden spoon or the rolling pin, but how many modern Scottish households have goffering irons, fir-candle holders or bannock toasters as anything except ornaments? When a folk tale loses its entertainment value it is either changed or taken out of circulation for a while. But if the story or any of its motifs regain their relevance you can guarantee that the storytellers will take it up again. This is as true today as it has always been.[6] Similarly, when people grow tired of a game they will stop playing it or change it. I once saw a small group of girls skipping. Their rhyme started as a traditional Essex one about a girl who is born, grows, falls in love, marries, has children . . . But in their rhyme the woman then got divorced and fought for custody of the children before dying – a particularly clear case of a game adjusting to a modern setting. All games (and particularly those used in Social Drama) are alive and responding to the needs and wishes of the people playing them.

I constantly hear adults and older children lamenting that all the old games ('the real games') have died out. The Opies,[7] among others, have proved that this simply isn't true. We just don't know where to look to see them being played, or we find it difficult to accept that a game may have gone out of popularity for a while and is just waiting for a chance to return. Games will return and change as long as people want to play them and as long as they benefit (knowingly or unknowingly) from doing so. They will survive for as long as they are entertaining and useful.

If we examine games in their traditional settings we can often identify functions of adult play which are just as useful as those we have been looking at in children. Many of these functions are actually the same, as the faculties developed in children's games need constantly to be exercised if we are not to atrophy. Sociability, for example, is not something you can finally qualify in at the age of thirteen. It takes a lifetime to learn. Just as physical muscles need to be exercised so do our social, emotional and intellectual muscles. Games do this for us no matter how old we are.[8]

The most obviously functional games are those which involve a particular practical skill. Archery must surely have developed as a way of teaching and improving hunting skills. Games of strength like arm-wrestling and the many traditional pain-endurance tests obviously have a long history, as do the common games which help to develop dexterity. The riddle, the conundrum, the joke and the pun are all types of traditional material which exercise the intellect, the wit and the creative drive. There are many games which rely on counting (and not merely for scoring). Many of them are board games which go back for hundreds, even thousands of years.[9] In them there is a constant, often complex manipulation of space, size, number, and permutations – all sorts of intellectual juggling.

We have noted earlier that children's games-playing often has a ritualistic element, and this is true of some adult play too. Rituals are repeated actions and events that have some extra, often symbolic meaning for the participants. There are many examples of traditions which mix ritual and play, including the celebratory games played only at particular times of the year (Saints' days, festivals, carnivals and the turn of the seasons). Many of them are loaded with symbolism; they are fertility rites, calls for the return of the summer, celebrations of the harvest, a declaration of unity with the earth and the universe. Not that the players would necessarily tell you this. The 'reason' is forgotten (if it was ever known) and the 'explanation' unimportant. But the playing is vital.

The simplest function of ritual is the regulation of life's uncertainties, but it can also be used to facilitate social bonding, to act as a form of communal expression or to mark the progress from one stage of life to another.[10] There are games played at birthdays, weddings and even funerals. The traditional Irish wake was a time not only for mourning the dead but for celebrating life and the living. There were games galore[11] and many of them have travelled with the folk and turned up in Canadian parlours and Australian outposts as well as in Social Drama workshops.

Adults play games the world over and there is sometimes an element of social control in their playing. The Inuit of North America, for example, play games like Muk (see game 39) in the depths of winter to pass the long winter hours. In doing so they can divert and defuse some of the internecine conflicts that arise when a group live so closely and so perilously.

Modern fool's errands (of which I am starting a collection) have a social function, too, and it is one that Social Drama has adopted. Apprentices and raw recruits have long been the butt of their workmates' playful cruelty. They are sent to the stores to ask for striped paint, left-handed hammers, skirting ladders (for climbing up skirting boards) and elbow grease. I have heard of one nursing auxiliary who was sent for a set of fallopian tubes. Some newcomers are sent off to ask for what sounds like 'a long weight' and they can stand outside an office door for several minutes before realizing what the joke has been. The fool's errand has become a traditional part of apprenticeship. It acts as a sort of initiation rite (you only fall for them once) after which you are one of the group and can be involved in fooling the next arrival. The carefully controlled use of the 'trick' game has become a regular part of Social Drama, too. Humour is a great leveller and can cut equanimously through all sorts of barriers.

The fact that people play games without openly acknowledging these (and other) functions is not important. We do all sorts of things without knowing why. And if this functional analysis of games seems dry it is important to point out that it is not meant to detract our attention from the most important element of games: fun. It would be fatuous to analyse games purely in terms of their hidden significance, and indeed there are many games which are only played for the amusement they afford. But Social Drama demands at least an instinctive belief that the games, as traditional material, are, and always have been, useful.

ENJOYMENT AS THE ESSENTIAL MOTIVATOR (B.A.)

Social Drama would fail, miserably, if it was not enjoyed by all, but, strange as it may seem, some people are actually suspicious of enjoyment. There has long been a half-baked belief that learning should not be fun. Teachers and laymen can be critical of the enjoyment which children find in Creative Drama lessons, whilst the teachers who conduct the lessons can be exhilarated by the group dynamics which are released. The excitement, and positive human involvement lead to vitality and a highish, conversational noise level; something which is not normally expected in school. One of the problems in conducting social drama sessions with teenagers, or adults, is that they are likely to see the situation as a school class. All the restraints which they knew in school come into operation again. The only way to counteract this is to ensure that the group feels absolutely secure: allow a great deal of socializing at the outset, and encourage people to lose themselves in purposeful play. It is important that they should soon realize that the stern voice of command will not be heard, but that with their co-operation, they will be led. The leader must not seem to have a premium of knowledge, and mystique; all she has to have are good 'fun ideas'. But this is not to say that she must be weak, there are times when the whole group has to be brought under control; at these times the sturdy, velvet glove should be used, rather than the iron-clad fist.

Enjoyment has been the aim in all Social Drama sessions we have been associated with, and in most cases this has been achieved, but there are exceptions. You cannot command people to enjoy themselves, that would be rather like the priest who hits the boy over the head with the Bible, and tells the boy to pray louder. A few people are so unwilling to play that they mentally withdraw at the outset. Extrovert loners are also difficult, but I have found that these non-co-operators are only a small minority. The following example illustrates how one such person might operate:– I was conducting a one-day course for people working in Social Services. This was part of a one-year course where the participants were aiming at a Final Certificate. There was, therefore, some pressure on the group to co-operate, and to see the values of Social Drama. Most of the group got off to a good start, but I noticed that one man seemed to be rather withdrawn. He was not shy; it was just that he seemed detached from any of the practical exercises we were undertaking. There were several breaks for people to question the use, or value, of what we were doing, but he did not raise any objections in front of the group. During the lunch break he was approached by a girl student who was helping me. He was prepared to tell her that he did not wish to be involved in any of the games, or drama activities, but that he did wish to know all about them so that he could conduct sessions of his own. The nub of what he was saying was contained in a final remark; that grown adults could not be expected to enjoy the sort of things we were doing. He could neither enjoy nor play. Whether this man would ever make a good session leader is open to debate. He may well have been able to enthuse people by the sheer force of his personality, but our general advice to anyone who has tried and failed to find their *own* enjoyment in Social Drama would be that they are better to use another medium for their work with other people.

The principal motive for Social Drama is to encourage and enable an awakening through fun. Genuine laughter must occur quite early, but it is not only laughter which indicates enjoyment; the enthusiasm with which people throw themselves into the activities is another. We know that in all walks of life we are more committed to the tasks we find enjoyable. Enjoyment and motivation stimulate each other and both are essential components of success.

The central core of Social Drama must be social games, but almost any subject can, and does, crop up outside these. The leaders, and the group, must be prepared to turn in any direction when this is required. We have known sessions where mathematic problems were resolved; social problems were explored; where dances were improvised; where plays were invented; where simulation exercises were undertaken; where stories were told; where masks were worn; where the whole group has gone into the street, to get reactions of the public; and where nothing at all has happened, except talking. But in every successful session we have known, there has been the all-pervading sense of shared experience and communal enjoyment.

CREATING NEW GAMES (R. W.)

One of the delights for a Social Drama leader is to watch her group inventing a new game. Another is to rediscover an old favourite in a new setting, played differently, perhaps, and often with a new name. These are signs that the games are as alive in the workshops as they are in the playground, on the village green or in an Inuit settlement.

If we accept that games are traditional material, we must create the sort of environment in which such material can grow, survive and be adapted. This is not as awesome as it may sound, for the Social Drama workshop (when it is working well) is already a fairly good approximation. The people are gathered together to explore the subject of man. There is the 'older generation' (the leaders and possibly the people who have attended before) who are going to encourage and enable the exploration. There is the 'younger generation' who are going to use the material if they like it and who will change it or dispense with it if it doesn't suit their purpose or their taste. There is the sensation of a shared growth through common aims and individual objectives. There is a strong sense of control over the content and purpose of the session. All these contribute to the creativity needed to generate new ideas.

Any leader who has a fundamental belief in the material and processes of Social Drama will not find it hard to make up new games to try out with the group. Think of the games that go well, the experiences that the group respond to, the sort of things that you and the group would like to happen . . . and a germ of an idea will be formed. Often the best time to do this is in the session itself, particularly when the group seems open to new ideas. Be prepared to try a variation of a favourite game, or after something has gone well try it again but with a new rule, a new context, a new intention. Read the games in this book and in the works in the bibliography and think of changing them. Be prepared to discuss the changes with your group, to try them out and to ask for suggestions. Do not be depressed if a new game does not work – it may set off something else. Be inventive, be open, be responsive and encourage the same features in your group and their play. Sometimes you will have to adapt a game for the specific demands or limitations of your group. This problem is dealt with in the relevant sections of Chapter 4, but it does stress the point that any leader must always remember: it is the *group*'s needs and wishes that are paramount.

The boundaries of Social Drama are very flexible, and are mainly determined by what the leaders and group members are happy to explore. For ourselves we can think of very few environments where we would be against trying Social Drama. We have ambitions of running sessions in Parliament and local government as well as in hospitals, schools, community centres and bars. The important point is that *you* can use Social Drama as an adjunct to whatever you are already doing or are prepared to do. The sessions are 'liberal studies' in the widest possible sense. They are the study of self and others by practice and observation, action and reaction. Wherever and whenever people are involved in that study Social Drama has a part to play. We will be looking at specific applications in Chapter 4, but first we would like to examine the nature and problems of leadership and offer some general guidance on the planning, organization and management of workshops.

Notes

1 Karl Groos, 'The Play of Animals: Play and Instinct' in J. S. Bruner, A. Jolly, and K. Sylva, eds., *Play: Its Role In Development and Evolution* (Harmondsworth: Penguin, 1976). This book contains a wealth of other philosophical, scientific and literary studies of play and is an ideal starting point for the reader wishing to explore this area more thoroughly.

2 P. and I. Opie, *Children's Games in Street and Playground* (Oxford: Oxford University Press, 1969), p. 2.

3 Eric Berne, *Games People Play* (Harmondsworth: Penguin, 1968), pp. 116–20.

4 P. Brook, *The Empty Space* (Harmondsworth: Pelican, 1972), p. 46.

5 For discussion and illustrations of the use of traditional material in a therapeutic context see R. Watling, 'Folklore and Ritual as a Basis for Personal Growth and Therapy' in B. Warren, ed., *Using the Creative Arts in Therapy* (London: Croom Helm, 1984).

6 Anyone who doubts the existence or extent of the modern folk tale, or its reliance on age-old ideas should read J. H. Brunvand, *The Vanishing Hitchhiker: Urban Legends and Their Meanings* (London: Pan, 1983).

7 Opies, *Children's Games in Street and Playground*, pp. 5–6, 16.

8 It is important to note that I am not talking here about organized competitive sports. They have their values, of course, but they are not ultimately concerned with the sorts of personal and social developments dealt with by Social Drama.

9 For details of the history of boardgames and illustrations that can actually be played as the originals see B. Love, *Play the Game* (London: Michael Joseph, 1978) and R. C. Bell, *The Boardgame Book* (London: Marshall Cavendish, 1979).

10 The original, if somewhat outdated account of these particular rituals is A. Van Gennep, *The Rites of Passage* (Boston and London: Routledge, 1960).

11 See S. O'Suilleabhain, *Irish Wake Amusements* (Cork: Mercier, 1969).

SECTION II
SOCIAL DRAMA IN ACTION

3. The Problems of Leadership
(B.A. & B.W.)

Social Drama, in common with many artistic and creative activities, can happen virtually anywhere and at any time; all it requires is a group of people and a space. However, for that meeting to have shape and purpose, and to prevent the meeting degenerating into either an apathetic impasse, with everyone just waiting for someone to suggest or do something; or into a free-for-all with everyone scrambling to get their ideas heard, the group needs some form of leadership. This leadership can take many forms but in the initial stages Social Drama needs direction if it is to be successful.

The relationship between the leader and his group is crucial to the development of those engaged in Social Drama. The leader must set the tone of the session and create a safe environment in which the group members can be themselves without fear of danger or retribution from others. To be successful the leader has to create a bridge between the material at his command (i.e. his store of games, ideas and activities) and the personal needs and beliefs of the people participating in the session. In Social Drama the leader's primary function is to enable participants to work at their own pace, enjoy themselves and achieve success; not the earth-shattering successes that change the shape of world history but those little everyday successes that we all need in order to survive and grow in our impersonal western society.

The ways that each leader creates an environment which he feels will facilitate success for his group can be as different as the leaders themselves. In Social Drama there are as many ways to lead as there are leaders. Leadership is a truly personal experience. It is based on the unique relationship each leader creates with his world, and leadership styles are shaped by the blending of personal philosophy, experience and skill with the quality and diversity of material available. In fact the most valuable commodity at each leader's disposal is what he takes into the room: that is himself. We three have shared many experiences. In particular we have often been together when we have first been exposed to a new game or idea. In almost every instance we have used that information slightly differently because, while we shared the same experiences, we are significantly different people.

The concepts of *start from where you are*,[1] and *make new material your own* are perhaps the first two 'basic rules' that a leader needs to know. These two form the framework on which we feel a new leader should operate. However, the realities of everyday interactions also require that the leader be flexible and ready to change his style of leadership to meet the changing needs of the group. Unfortunately some leaders treat their style of leadership like a favourite coat. Something that they put on to run a session, never changing it unless it becomes threadbare and starts to fall apart. They fail to remember, or perhaps never realized, that a good leader must always be adapting to the changes in the working environment. To an extent a good leader is able to exercise some degree of control in the regulation of his environment but it is also strongly affected by such things as the weather, the mood of the group and the activities he presents to them. One favourite coat is not sufficient for all occasions. Far better to have a large wardrobe at his disposal and a frame of mind that does not prevent him being a quick-change artist so that he can successfully meet the possible mercurial changes in his working environment.

Whilst some people might argue that good leaders are born not made there are those of us who still believe that natural ability can be helped to see the light of day. We are not convinced that everyone can be taught to be a good leader but there are a number of ways that individuals desiring to become leaders can learn some of the necessary basic skills. There are perhaps three major routes by which leaders learn their craft – apprenticeship/tutelage, practicum, and the 'deep end plunge'. Each route has its strengths and its weaknesses.

Apprenticeship is when a student learns from a tutor in the work setting. The tutor acts as a mentor to her pupil and the pupil acts as the mentor's assistant, learning the craft of leadership 'on the job' from an 'expert' in that field. Working 'one-to-one' with an experienced leader helps to provide valuable insight into the process of leadership but like the study of just one style of Kung Fu it can also provide a one-sided view of the art. Unless the mentor is both eclectic in approach and an exceptional human being there is a tendency for her to provide extremely valuable but often limited experience for her pupils. Rob and I were extremely lucky to have had such a far-sighted and multitalented man as Bert for our mentor, but as we would all acknowledge there is no way a single human being can have all the answers.

Another approach for prospective leaders is to enrol in a training programme which contains a practicum component. This training programme might be carried out through a post-secondary educational establishment (e.g. a university or college) or it might be attached to a clinical institution (e.g. a hospital). Each training scheme is different but in general there

is more than one tutor to learn from and the practical component of instruction is usually outweighed by the theoretical
components. The student has more role models to learn from
but a far more impersonal learning environment and less time
spent working with each mentor. The tendency is to provide
students with a wide-ranging theoretical 'raison d'être' but little
depth of practical experience. The end result is that students
know what should happen but are perhaps short on the
experience of how to make these expected results occur.

All too often leaders have to learn their craft by jumping in at
the deep end. The leader who decides, or is compelled to take
this course of action may end up a very strong and resourceful
swimmer or she may be so scared by the experience that she
vows never to swim again. However, every leader has ultimately to take the plunge. To have had practice, through apprenticeship or practicum training, is obviously a valuable asset but at
some point the water wings have to come off and the novice
must learn to swim by herself. She has to learn to make spur-of-
the-moment decisions, trusting to her intuition, and she has to
respond to these as she thinks fit. The leader who has learnt by
taking 'the deep end plunge' and has successfully survived those
first initial encounters may be as well-qualified a leader as
anyone else. She will certainly have had first-hand practical
experience; however, she will be short of ideas from outside her
own experience. Luckily more and more 'mentors' are commit-
ting their ideas to paper and many first-rate practitioners are
running intensive training workshops to help furnish leaders
with new ideas and practical approaches. All these new experiences must be handled in the light of the two basic rules outlined
previously but they do give valuable insight into other leader's
philosophies and successful working practices. These then need
to be matched to the individual's capabilities and the needs of

the group she is leading. This is difficult at first but through observation, assimilation and processing of the multitude of human interactions and responses that you witness as a leader of Social Drama, this slowly becomes second nature to you.

The rest of this chapter is devoted to providing leaders and prospective leaders of Social Drama sessions with a few of the authors' own ideas and methods of working. We examine the problems of leadership in three phases: those initial problems faced in planning sessions for new groups; those problems related to developing social drama with the same group over long periods of time (including the thorny questions of dependency); and those problems related to the leader's own personal development, particularly in maintaining the freshness of the material for the leader and the group.

FIRST STEPS

Nearly every leader has at least one person who has acted as an inspiration or a model for the way she works. This person more often than not has positive qualities that she admires, can see in his work, and aspire to recreate in her own. While imitation is possibly the greatest form of flattery it is not necessarily the best form of leadership. What the new leader often forgets is that everyone, even the 'heroes'' had to start somewhere. The person you admire is an experienced achiever, someone who has learnt from his mistakes and successes, and who works from a vast reservoir of stored ideas, activities and experience. These are resources that the novice does not yet have. To simply copy the style of those people you admire is to be like the art student who copies the style of the later works of Picasso without understanding how and why these 'abstract' techniques evolved.

Given time all leaders build up their own stored experiences which will slowly give meaning to each individual's process of leadership, making that process uniquely their own.

There are no hard and fast rules to leading creative sessions such as Social Drama. There are no panaceas; no lesson plans which can be used to ensure a session's success. Each group of individuals, each leader, is far too different for us to be able to provide a definite road map which guarantees results. What we can do is to provide guidelines, road signs if you like, with which you can chart your own path, take your own road and hopefully gain some notion of where you are now and where you are going. The guidelines may not be complete maps but it is hoped they will at least help the new leader gain some feel for the speed, direction and final destination of that particular journey. They may not prevent you from going off course but hopefully they will enable you to find your way back with the minimum of fuss and delay.

It may be a small consolation, but every leader has faced the same problem. Just like the driver who has only practised on a simulator we each have to get into the car and deal with the reality of other cars, traffic hazards and adverse weather conditions. In the first few sessions of leadership we are all faced with the question of 'why things aren't working as it says they should in the manual' yet slowly the whole process becomes second nature and we eventually wonder what all the fuss was about in the first place.

These guidelines are intended for the new leader and for the leader starting work with a new group. No matter how experienced you are, work with a new group or individual requires a return to basic principles although the more experience you gain the shorter this reconsideration becomes. As Social Drama can be used in a wide variety of settings these guidelines refer only to the initial stages of leadership. In Chapter 4 the specific needs of particular groups are discussed in more detail.

GUIDELINES FOR LEADERSHIP

- *Good preparation is the key to success.* So take time to do your homework.
- Make sure you find out who you are working with. Take the time to meet the individual(s) before planning the session, if at all possible, as this human contact fleshes out second-hand reports. Make sure you know:
    - The number in the group
    - The individual's age/sex and name
    - Roughly what each individual's capabilities are
    - About any major physical limitations (e.g. speech)
    - Whether anyone has any previous experience of Social Drama or other creative activities
- Make sure you know what, if anything, is expected from you. Social Drama can be employed in a variety of settings and for a variety of reason. The 'contract'[2] between yourself, the group and your employer should be established before starting a session of Social Drama.
- *Always plan for the needs of your group.* Try to take account not only of the personal needs of the individual(s) you are working with but also the physical limitations of the space/environment in which the sessions occur.
- Try to choose a room that meets your requirements. For a group of about 20–25 people it should be about 30ft × 30ft. Anything smaller will limit free movement. Conversely, a room with the proportions of a school assembly hall is too

overwhelming for early work, although such a space may be useful later on.

- The atmosphere of the room needs to be relaxing; more like a lounge than a classroom. Often rooms in old buildings are more restful than those in clinical, modern complexes, although peeling paint and sagging wallpaper present as much of a distraction as sterile white rooms.
- The ambience of the room is probably more important than its size.
- *In practice you have to learn to make do with any room.* We have never turned down the offer to run a session in what, at first sight, might seem an unsuitable room. Bert runs regular sessions with a local club for stroke victims in a long narrow room. It is so narrow that when the people are lined up in their wheelchairs there is only about 6 feet between them. In an even more unusual occurrence two of us were once asked to do a Social Drama training session for marriage guidance counsellors at a regional conference. Neither of us had seen the proposed venue beforehand but we had been warned that it was of an awkward shape, on two levels and that upwards of 60 people were expected for the session. On our arrival we were shown into the room, which was like a corridor, with the delegates, all standing drinking coffee, and filling the whole space. After a quick discussion we rearranged our plans choosing activities we felt would work under such, almost impossible conditions. Everyone seemed to enjoy the session and we still meet people who remark on how much they gained from it.
- *All one really needs for Social Drama to take place is a group and a space.* However, from time to time some or all of the following 'props' may be found useful to a session:
  - Chairs   – enough to seat the whole group

- A table — to hold tape recorder/record player, to spread out props or hold written work
- Record player or tape recorder
- Rostra/stage blocks — to alter levels
- Lights — the ability to black out room or vary light levels can be very helpful
- Costume — old hats, simple tunics etc.
- Parachute or a double/king size sheet
- Newspaper, string, paper, card and scissors
- Balloons — a variety of sizes and colours
- Piano, tambourine or other instruments
- Felt pens, chalk pastels
- Soft balls — various sizes (e.g. tennis, football)
- Objets d'art — to stimulate the imagination (e.g. old bag, antique camera)

- Try to make sure you have at least some of the above props on hand. It is amazing what results can occur and how many new ideas will arise.
- Try to prepare a rough order of events. A cue card with a list of games on it works well. Make sure you have more than enough games for the session.
- Make sure you let the group know beforehand what clothing will be suitable for that session. Generally loose, comfortable clothing is what is needed for Social Drama (e.g. loose-fitting jeans and tee-shirt or jogging suit). Some people come to a session straight from their professional obligations, whilst others will be dressed in the latest dance fashions — purple-striped leotard and all. However, it is possible to run very successful sessions regardless of the clothing being worn — a notable occasion comes to mind. Two of us were once invited to run a session of Social Drama at a curriculum development conference for college

lecturers. Despite a request from us, all 40 participants were wearing their 'Sunday best'. Very quickly those be-suited ladies and gentlemen made it very clear that while they were willing to participate they were certainly *not* going to do anything that might sully their attire. After a quick discussion we selected activities which were non-threatening to their clothing, and the session then proceeded very smoothly and successfully.

- When planning early sessions try to eliminate activities which might cause embarrassment or put people at social risk. *Remember that your work is directed towards building confidence, trust and self-awareness in the hope that participants in Social Drama will find it easier to cope with social situations.*
- *Start off slowly.* There is no rush.
- Don't try and rush through activities. Some games won't work. Just move on to the next one. Others will be a surprising success, so don't move on simply because you want to get through your material. *Adjusting your pace to the needs of the group comes with time and practice.*
- *Introduce yourself* – let the group get a sense of who you are but don't tell them too much about what you have planned as this might build up expectations or misapprehensions.
- *Play name games to start each session* – being on first-name terms is of great advantage. Even if the group is drawn from a large organization and the boss is present with the office boy or the headmaster with his pupils, being on first-name terms helps to create a good working atmosphere.
- *Plan activities which are reassuring and enjoyable.* Having established who the members of the group are with a name game don't send them back into their shell with activities that 'put them on the spot'.
- *Always start each activity at the beginning.* There is a tendency,

particularly when working with a new group, to start at the point you finished last time and not at the beginning. This assumes knowledge and experience that the new group doesn't possess. This can lead to frustration and disappointment for everyone concerned.

– *Introduce each new activity clearly and concisely.* When speaking, try to take account of the language capabilities of your group, using the simplest, most appropriate words. Try to find suitable metaphors and images which enable you to rephrase the instructions. Give visual reinforcement and gestural clues, wherever this seems appropriate. Finally, if it seems necessary, do a quick demonstration before asking the group to participate in a new activity.

– *Always allow individuals the option to opt out of an activity.* If an individual does choose this route *don't* just leave them to themselves. Check if they might like to join the next game and possibly even the one they initially declined but, in the first sessions, don't force anyone to do something they don't want to.

– *Try to give shape to the session.* Start slowly, warming up participants for the workshop. Whatever the development of the session make sure you include a time for unwinding at the end. This may be an activity such as one of the relaxation exercises or it may simply be time to talk over a cup of tea or coffee before the participants go home.

– *Social Drama should be conducted with firmness but there is no room for authoritarianism.* Try to lead by example making sure people know that you are prepared to participate and that you are not simply going to bark directions from the sidelines.

– *Always remain observant.* Keeping your eyes and ears open is essential to the accurate observation of the group process.

Attempt to meet the moment-by-moment needs of individuals as they arise.

- *Relax and enjoy yourself.* Remember a key to the success of Social Drama is the element of fun and enjoyment which enables participants to 'exceed themselves'. If you aren't enjoying the session it's unlikely that anyone else is *but* this does not mean that you should be enjoying yourself at the expense of the participants. *Always remember who the session is for.*
- At the end of each session *take time to reflect on the events of the day*. Ideally keep a journal – not just of the activities which made up the session but also the responses of the participants. It is a good idea to note your own feelings towards the activities and the group in here as well. This journal will become invaluable when developing Social Drama with a particular group over a long period of time.

THE DEVELOPMENT OF SOCIAL DRAMA – SUSTAINING THE GROUP'S INVOLVEMENT OVER TIME

The problems faced by a leader in the initial stages of Social Drama are eventually replaced by different concerns. The focus shifts from the development of a rapport with the group and getting to know them, to the question of how to sustain interest in the activities and continue to meet the changing needs of the participants. Ultimately, the leader may have to come to terms with the fact that an individual, or in some cases a whole group, can no longer benefit from the skills, expertise and activities that are on offer; a point where the leader's contract has to be totally reviewed and in some instances brought to an end.

- *Repetition is the key to success*[3] – Having survived the first few hurdles (i.e. meeting the group for the first time, running the first session, having the group agree to come back for further sessions, etc.), it is important to make them feel at home. Try to include successful, reassuring material in the next few sessions – activities that the group enjoyed and requested. Try to let the group feel that the first session was not just a flash in the pan but that your meetings will continue to be successful and enjoyable interactions.

- *Introduce new activities slowly.* Don't swamp participants with new games. Always allow them the chance to see familiar landmarks. *As a safety net, wherever possible, plan to follow a new activity with a tried and tested old gem* at least early on in the group's development.

- Get to know your material inside-out. Where and from whom you learnt a game or exercise doesn't matter. What you must seek to do is to make each game your own – *you must learn to be able to write each game or exercise in your own 'hand writing' and not simply copy the style of your teacher.*

- You should have a surfeit of games and drama exercises. There should be enough variety in your material to enable a quick change of emphasis when it is required. As our great friend and colleague Bill Morris often remarked, *"Always expect the unexpected."* This attitude of 'whatever happens I can cope' helps to establish a flexible and relaxed style, for in Social Drama, as in other creative areas, the unexpected may prove a fabulous catalyst for generating new games and activities.

- *Work towards increasing the group's involvement in the decision-making and leadership process.* This might go through stages of development but once a sense of group identity has been established, try to be flexible enough to allow any member to take the lead. Initially this will probably mean somebody leading one game, perhaps her favourite or possibly a new one she brought to the group. However, over a period of time the members of the group may take more and more responsibility for leading the sessions, particularly in the area of developing new material for the group's use.

- *As the group develops you may well find yourself spending more time listening and talking and less time involved in activities.* It is often a mistake to feel that you have to be providing games and activities. Often the discussion is the most valuable part of the session. As the group feels comfortable with you they may also feel able to open up and share their feelings and problems with you individually or as a whole group. This may be threatening and uncomfortable for some leaders and it is essential that you try to be aware of your own limitations and fears. If you have studied with an instructor or a mentor this should have been part of your training. However, whether you had this self-awareness component included in your training or not, it is important that you establish your own listening network (see next section in this chapter).

- Social Drama, unlike psychodrama, does not lend itself well to dealing with problems head on, a more circuitous route needs to be charted. It is best to work slowly towards any 'in-depth' work that is to be approached. However, as was intimated in the last paragraph, often the group determines the depth of leader/group interactions – personal revelations may be shared with you in the first two or three sessions, much later on in the group's development or not at all. Never force an issue onto anyone.

- In the final analysis sustaining a group's interest and developing its involvement with Social Drama depends very heavily on the leader's remaining fresh and alive to the participants involved in the sessions (i.e. the leader himself and the group members) and the games and exercises that make up the material. This process of 'staying alive' is the subject of the last section of this chapter.

STAYING ALIVE

There are many skills a leader needs to cultivate, some of these come naturally and others have to be worked at. Whatever the degree of difficulty specific leadership skills present they are honed on our first-hand experience.

- A leader can be thought of as part detective/part balancing act; the detective always observant, weighing up information being given her by the group and then trying to balance all these pieces of information – strengths and weaknesses of individuals, current moods, feelings etc. – with the activities and games at her command, always taking into account experiences from past situations.
- *Reflect on the 'successes' and 'failures' of each session.* Make use of your journal to record your own changing feelings so as to come to terms with the possible roots of these experiences.
- *Build up a support network of friends and professional colleagues that you can discuss problems with.* Far too often leaders are isolated, making decisions on their own, sometimes resulting in a belief in their own infallibility – this is not healthy for the leader or the group.
- *Take the time to gain new experiences.* Go to other leaders' sessions, go to workshops, evening classes, the theatre, anything that exposes you to new ideas and activities.

Social Drama thrives on diversity so strive for divergent experiences – you wouldn't want to eat steak every night or else your palate would be bored – any new experience will expand your horizons but classes in Art, Yoga, Dance, Music or Video for example may well complement your work in Social Drama.

- *Keep up with any relevant literature.* It's not always easy to keep reading especially if you have a busy schedule and a family to look after. However, it is important to supplement practical experiences with theoretical developments and case studies from this and complementary fields of study. This is particularly important for people working in large institutions as a lot of a leader's time will probably be spent defending and justifying your work to others (particularly administrators) who will constantly want reminding why it is worth paying you for what you do.

- *Take the time to relax.* No matter how many new experiences you take in you need time to simply switch off and relax. This is one of the most essential parts of refilling your cup.

- As Roberta Nadeau says *"you can't pour from an empty cup"* – so keep yourself fit and well. All leadership is physically, mentally and emotionally demanding. It is essential that you keep yourself at the peak of your abilities – this is *not* a plea for the body beautiful but it is important that you keep yourself at *your* optimum fitness. Everyone expects you to be on top of your form and there are rarely any allowances made for your feeling under the weather. It may be a better move to phone in sick than to carry on in the face of a minor illness as mistakes can easily be made.

- *Avoid confrontation wherever possible.* Try to keep your finger on the pulse of the situation and try to diffuse or control volatile situations before they get out of hand. The important word is control. Leadership inevitably brings with it a number of explosive or emotional situations but these remain manageable if you shape the situation and don't let the situation shape you.

— *Be aware of the different means at your disposal for reshaping a potentially volatile situation and be particularly conscious of the different 'sticks and carrots' that each individual responds to.* Whilst constructive criticism, positive reinforcement and insight may be what you like to use some people require you to raise your voice before they will give you any attention. As a leader you must be sensitive and sympathetic to an individual's predicament and personality, sometimes using covert means to deal with the problem through metaphor, analogy or reframing of the behaviour, and sometimes dealing with the problem head-on by identification and discussion of the problem with the person concerned. *Always be aware of your 'contract', training and abilities.* If you feel, for one or other reason, that the problem you are being presented with is beyond your capabilities or responsibilities seek advice and help from qualified professionals. There is nothing more dangerous than simply muddling through because you feel you ought to. This is true for the person presenting the problem as well as for your development as a leader.

— *Try to treat each situation as a unique event dealing with matters as they arise and on their own merits.* As you become more experienced there is a tendency to fall back on 'types' seeing interactions or behaviour in terms of previous experience and using 'plan 42b' to deal with it. This is when past experience acts as a block rather than a catalyst for the organic interaction essential to personal and group development. By using this approach the leader can become a machine working on automatic pilot and simply going through the motions.

— *Be patient and don't be afraid to let time pass.* Busy time is the enemy of creative Social Drama. Give slower members of the group the time to succeed without being cajoled or criticized by their colleagues; this will require the development of a sympathetic and supportive attitude amongst group members. An equally difficult problem is those people who are forever hogging the stage wishing to be the centre of attention. Volunteers are often essential for the development of new games but you should be careful to ration out 'favoured' roles amongst the whole of the assembled company. Sometimes you may have to speak directly to the individual concerned. A particular instance comes to mind of a young man involved in a group in Shrewsbury who eventually had to be asked to leave because his exhibitionist tendencies were getting in the way of the rest of the group's development and in one particular instance, where he started to strip in front of the assembled company, his behaviour was offensive to the other members of the group who were all aged between 17 and 26. This was an extreme example but there have been many other occasions where an individual's need to be the centre of attention has been detrimental to his and others' development, each had to be dealt with as the situation and the personality of the individuals demanded.

— *Always try to remain flexible and open to new ideas.* ('Go with the flow') – the ability to think on your feet, to improvise and to allow games and activities to take the shape the group can relate to, are essential skills which come very slowly and, it could be argued, need to be re-learnt with

each new group.
- As time passes and the group continues to meet on a regular basis over long periods, be aware that you may be creating a need or dependency for the sessions. Individuals may want to keep coming long after Social Drama can be of real value to them or others in the group.
- In Shrewsbury, we were involved in a long-running regular session of Social Drama put on as part of the liberal studies programme offered to the local art school and technical college students. Many students continued to come to these sessions, long after they had left Shrewsbury, some travelling long distances just to be part of those Wednesday afternoon sessions. Some were extremely valuable additions to the group. They were able to help lead the sessions and provided 'peer' reinforcement for some new and unsure members. Others were a block to the group's development. They wanted the sessions to be exactly as they remembered and experienced them. As a result inadvertently, sometimes actively, they prevented the organic metamorphosis of games that is the creative life blood of the Social Drama process. They had perhaps subconsciously hoped that Social Drama would continue to fill certain gaps in their life but they no longer belonged to the group who were creating Social Drama at that time, in that place. They wanted the sessions to remain constant in their lives. It is a trap that leaders can fall into as well. This pitfall for leaders and participants is most likely to occur in educational institutions, where people attend Social Drama for a designated period of time (a term or a year) and when an individual stays on for an extra year and elects to participate in Social Drama for a second session.
- When working with special populations (see Chapter 4)

individuals may be encouraged by professional staff to remain within the group longer than is necessary. Often this professionally created dependency has more to do with safeguarding a professional's job than the needs of the disabled people involved in Social Drama.

– Your role with the group will probably change. You may begin to have doubts about your value to them. This may occur gradually as you allow individuals in the group slowly to take more and more responsibility for the shape and direction of the sessions, or it may come as a blinding flash of insight where you realize that an individual, or individuals, no longer need to be part of Social Drama. However, *whilst individuals may no longer need the benefits of Social Drama they may decide they want to continue meeting with you as the leader because they enjoy the activities and the general social interactions of the group so much.* It is at this point that you will need to renegotiate your 'contract' with the group or individual(s) concerned.

– *Be aware of other avenues and opportunities open to you and to members of the group.* You may want to encourage certain individuals to proceed to other things (e.g. theatre training, training in drama therapy). You may want to reshape the group's structure to accommodate new needs. This might mean working on a specific project (e.g. helping participants take Social Drama to senior citizens in residential establishments or patients in hospitals). Or you might organize the sessions more like a self-help group where you provide the space for them to meet and then look in on the group when they ask you to. These are but a couple of alternatives for the creative offshoots and developments of Social Drama.

– *Finally, never be afraid to say 'No'. Continue to have the courage* to say 'Stop' and always be prepared to admit when you are wrong. If you remain constant and fair in all your dealings, make the sessions enjoyable, interesting and stimulating, you are more than likely going to enjoy your work, be appreciated by those you come in contact with and continue to stay 'alive', creative and healthy.

Notes

1 Although not the first person to make this point, Brian Way does make it very clearly and forcefully throughout his excellent book *Development Through Drama* (London: Longman, 1967).

2 The term 'contract' is used here in an informal sense. It is not something committed to paper. This concept of a contract is explored in more detail in B. Warren, ed., *Using the Creative Arts in Therapy* (London: Croom Helm, 1984), pp. 9–13.

3 Grant Reddick, one of Bernie's colleagues at the University of Calgary, always used to tell this to his acting students. It is an obvious but wise maxim for any profession or area of study.

4. Working with Different Groups

We have each worked with a very wide variety of groups and individuals, though over the years we have also developed our own specific interests. In doing so we have discovered that there are certain fundamental rules of Social Drama which never change, irrespective of the composition of the group. Many of these have been covered in the last chapter and others are discussed in this one. These constants are mostly to do with the underlying assumptions that justify the work we do – a set of values if you like – which start with an unshakeable belief that people matter.

Social Drama is more *ascriptive* than *prescriptive*. That is to say it does not tend to identify people's weaknesses and *prescribe* treatment, rather it is concerned with *ascribing* strengths and abilities to *everyone* and encouraging them to reach out for new horizons. These strengths and abilities are the ones which make us valued and valuable. They are the qualities which make people important to themselves and to others. We do not attempt to define what it is to be human, but we believe that whatever people *are*, they are *more so* when they are being creative and caring in the ways that Social Drama encourages. We most certainly do not believe that people are less human or less valuable because they are mentally handicapped, physically handicapped, emotionally disturbed, old, ill or in any way 'abnormal'.

But the practical process of working with (for example) social science students rather than emotionally disturbed adolescents is markedly different. This chapter looks at five particular types of Social Drama setting and examines some of the demands and pitfalls that might be encountered in each.

(A) WORKING WITH EDUCATIONAL DRAMA (B.A.)

To start with the young child, most of his play acting *is* Social Drama in its best sense. The teacher does not have any problem finding a way in. As Peter Slade has pointed out creative drama is a natural child art and it does for the small child what more structured Social Drama can do for adolescents. We do not need to prepare the infant for drama by introducing drama games for the simple reason that he will already be playing a series of games which he finds enjoyable and which we realize are developmental. When the creative drama takes place in a school – as opposed to the vast amount which goes on in the child's free time – all we need to do is to see that the right conditions for play are there.[1]

The simple fact is that once you have really understood the dynamic of child drama you have found the key to understanding the child mind, and the organizing of drama sessions becomes a most enjoyable experience. The only problem which arises is when the teacher, true to her calling, feels that she should be feeding in some factual information. Let no one doubt that there is a development from week to week but the children are doing the development themselves, with the teacher offering stimulation when and if imagination flags. The teacher's main task is to keep a record of obvious leaps in progress. Is David relating better to the other children, has Mary made a very positive contribution etc. In doing this we are in the fashionable business of profiling.

Drama is so completely absorbing and charged that it is easy to structure child drama towards other areas of learning, and this has been the tendency in recent years. I find no fault with this side benefit so long as it is aimed at life, language and understanding people. The magic, the folk drive, the compulsive power of natural child drama would be reduced if any work was specifically geared towards a subject without human content. Stories from the history of mankind, or just good stories about people and what they do, can live through dramatization, and children can learn how we behave in different circumstances. We must also remember that in the child's world fairies, goblins and talking animals *exist*. The leaders and teachers of child drama should never forget that 'To study drama is to study life', and that Plato's thought on education is very apt: 'A Child Mind is a Fire to be Kindled, not a Vessel to be Filled'.

Where child drama is going to be encouraged indoors, with a teacher or play leader, the following provisions would be encouraging and helpful:– a medium-sized, comfortable room with a splinter-free floor, furnished with objects and props which the child would like to have in the play room. A few rostra blocks to allow different levels and climbing facilities; a dressing-up box; paints, pencils, crayons and paper; masks and make-up. It is an advantage if the room can be blacked out. (Some would disagree with this but children thrive on the opportunity to change or control the atmosphere.) Some simple spotlights should be provided; these should have colour filters because children can be inspired by coloured light. There should be simple musical instruments, especially percussive ones, and facilities for making their own with beans, tins, boxes, bottles and almost any junk which can make a sound. Sometimes the drama session turns, in an unplanned way, into a music session or even a dancing session but this is a bonus for cashing in on spontaneity. Where teachers are working in open-plan schools much valuable activity is bound to be restricted.

The teacher/leader is there in an advisory capacity and is mostly a sympathetic observer, but it is necessary to support the children and to give guidance when it is asked for. There are times when it is useful to be able to turn the play in a more positive direction. One must be prepared to take an active part in the play when asked to do so. Another way in is for the teacher to start off the proceedings by adopting a very definite acting role and then to allow the play to develop with this character as a catalyst.

Discipline problems can occur when some children 'act about' instead of acting with a purpose. This is likely to happen with those children who have been kept on too tight a rein from their first year in school. Not to put too fine a point on it they have already suffered from bad teaching practice. Another discipline problem is caused if any one child tries to dominate the group; such a child is likely to be behaving in a way which is meant to impress teacher. On the other hand, a child might be showing off through his acting; in this case it is best for the teacher to observe him without seeing him. We have to be especially careful about diagnosis in all these cases.

Some teachers lay great stress on what they call 'warm-up' exercises. In my experience young children have very little need for these although adults might require them before doing similar work. The main consideration is to ensure that you have set up a situation in which children are really being stretched by what they are doing. There is always the danger that children will return again and again to an over-used dramatic situation. This will probably give them a sense of security but little else, but at least you have been alerted to the fact that there is some insecurity around. In working with young children there is almost a reversal of roles between teacher and child. The child is the demonstrator whilst the teacher is able to learn about the learning processes in action.

Some reference should be made to traditional children's games. These chanting, singing and dancing games are as old as time. They happen wherever a group of children get together; in the fields, in the streets, and finally in the school playground. What they cling to in these is powerful ritual, which in itself requires repetition. There is a temptation to use them and even teach them. The children will co-operate and go through the motions of the game, but the need to play them, and the root drive which caused them, is not there. Most folk art is a travesty when it is artificially introduced, and children's singing games are no exception.

Drama in the Secondary School

As children get older their needs in drama, as in everything else, are bound to change because they have the instinctive understanding that they are progressing towards the all-powerful adult world. I would like to qualify what I am going to say later by stating at the outset that I firmly believe that children throughout the whole range of the secondary school should have regular drama sessions. If this does not happen it is because they are being sacrificed on the altar of a rigid and misguided examination system.

Pupils from about the age of twelve to sixteen will still welcome drama sessions but the fact that they do enjoy them so much leads some teachers to believe that it cannot be good for them. The sessions should be structured towards conscious, inspirational creativity rather than the spontaneous creativity of earlier years. There will still be a place for the improvised play but the themes might have changed and the planning might be more sophisticated. I say that the themes might have changed but the teacher should not be horrified if some groups still choose a traditional nursery story to act out. They are finding safety in themes which they know, and let us not forget that many of us adults can become involved in pantomime. The need for ritual might now be even stronger and this is where some of the work with the older pupils could take the form of Social Drama. The games used should have a strong dramatic content.

There is a danger with this age group, as with younger children, that the teacher will cash in on the class's love of drama and only use the subject as a learning tool. Where this happens I call it 'dedramatizing of drama'. This leads us to the question, in general, as to whether drama should be taught or whether it should be allowed to happen in the right environment. The direct teaching of drama will almost certainly lead towards the pupils' wanting to explore the adult concept of 'a play', and by that they mean performing plays upon stages. Not all will want to do this, higher up the age range, and with the fun of creative drama gone, some will begin to opt out of the structured discipline which is replacing it. The goats become many and the few sheep find drama in any form so intriguing that they want to develop it to the point of finding a career in the theatre.

As a side issue there are many secondary schools where the heavy hand of the inter-form drama festival rests. Some of these schools do not have any drama classes as such, after the second year, and yet the Head suddenly announces to his startled staff

that the festival will take place in a few weeks' time. It is only by
a miracle that these events are not a total disaster, but to be
charitable the Head concerned seems to realize that drama
should be in there somewhere.

Most secondary schools stage public performances of plays
with older students, some of the latter being willing participants
and others being cajoled or blackmailed to take part. If you are
Head Boy or Head Girl it is difficult to refuse to take part even if
you feel unhappy about acting. Some school productions, under
these odd conditions, succeed in exciting the audience with a
true dramatic experience. Still greater in number are those
productions which under Peter Brook's definition would have
to be categorized as Deadly Theatre. A short passage referring
to Shakespeare production should illustrate what I mean. 'The
Deadly Theatre takes easily to Shakespeare. We see his plays
done by good actors in what seems to be a proper way – they
look lively and colourful, there is music and everyone is dressed
up, just as they are supposed to be in the best classical theatres.
Yet secretly we find it excruciatingly boring – and in our hearts
we either blame Shakespeare, or theatre as such, or even
ourselves.'[2]

All those responsible for play productions in schools would
do well to read 'The Empty Space' and take Peter Brook's
words to heart, for it is surely in schools that we should see
experiment, originality and daring. What we do not want to see
is a young cast aping a professional production which, in any
case, is now quite possibly dead.

In recent years C.S.E. and 'O'- and 'A'-level examinations in
drama have been introduced into secondary schools. This was
one way of ensuring that drama got on to the syllabus, but more
than that, it recognized that there were some students whose
aptitudes lay in that direction and who could benefit by such

practical and academic exploration. But drama in a secondary school should be much wider-based to give benefit to the non-specialists. Play productions together with a drama curriculum syllabus should be seen as only one small part of what the drama dynamic can do in a school. In the junior school it is rightly assumed that all children can benefit from creative drama; I also suggest that Social Drama can benefit all secondary pupils.

The principal advantages of using Social Drama in the later years of secondary education are to do with the fact that the seniors have often come full circle from the starting point of Creative Drama in the junior school. Many of them are ready to become involved in play again, but the discoveries they make through play are particular whereas very young children experiment with a more generalized form of life discovery. That is to say that to the young child life can be seen in terms of black and white; the older child might begin to recognize different shades of grey. Older children have a pressing need to assess their attitudes to society, and the attitudes of society to them. Many of them begin to feel at risk in matters of behaviour and inter-personal relationships. They are struggling to understand what behaviour society allows and accepts. They can easily swing between two extremes, one of too much licence and the other of too much caution. Social Drama gives an ideal opportunity for experiment with common features of life and an assessment of the results. Life can be seen as something to be grasped with confidence and good humour.

To conclude this section I would like to stress that the main difference between primary and secondary school drama is that of extent. In primary schools the main concern is improvised creative drama with very limited staging of plays before an audience – it is junior Social Drama in fact; in the secondary school the subject should range much more widely over improvisations, scripted plays, productions, academic study and Social Drama.

Social Drama in Further Education

We have now moved into the area of young adults who probably do not see drama as a recreational subject or even as a universal folk art. To many of them drama is acting; a special expertise which a few people have and most don't. They will be quite content to be part of an audience watching plays, otherwise they will concentrate their interest in other fields. It is whilst studying in further education that some people come to realize that they would like a career in the theatre and this knowledge seems to dawn upon them when they have already committed themselves to some other course. I have known several students who have made this discovery and after transferring themselves to a drama school or to a university drama department they have often done quite well. Some other students, with a slight hankering after drama, are able to join an amateur drama society within the college. The number of such groups appearing at the Edinburgh Festival and in the National Festival of Students proves that this is an option for many, but it is also underlining the belief that drama in college means plays upon stages, or in the arena, pub or street, or wherever there is a space to put on a play for an audience. There should be another recreational, social use for drama in its wider sense; drama of discovery and drama of personal development, but there still seems to be a shortage of people willing to organize this 'therapy for the normal' and it is difficult to convince some college authorities of the validity – even the great need – for this workshop to be made possible. It is hoped that this book might go some way towards putting matters right.

Social Drama is particularly valuable with students of this age, and most of them are able to see the obvious advantages of it. The practice of it might have been started at senior secondary school level where, as has been said, children learn to experiment with life situations and apply what they discover to their own lives. The older student is usually more captivated by Social Drama games-playing than the younger one; they can now feel completely at ease with it. At this age many students will readily admit that through the work they can make progress in matters of self-discovery.

Social Drama also encourages a healthy sense of good humour and this can lay the foundation for a happy, well adjusted personality in later life. If they have learnt to co-operate with others in a happy non-competitive way they are likely to cope more successfully in their occupational roles. The excessive rigidity one encounters among those in higher administrative posts, and even on committees could be modified in those who have made early peace with themselves in matters of relationships. Those who undertake and understand the techniques of Social Drama will readily accept their natural role-playing state. Our educational system has been dominated by subjects and examinations. Is it not time for us to encourage all students to study life as most drama students do?

In conclusion I am aware that this book is about Social Drama, and if at times I seem to have been straying into the area of theatre it is simply that all aspects of drama overlap, particularly in education. Theatre can never be successful if it remains bound up within its own conventions and know-how; it must constantly draw from life and the drama of life. Similarly, Social Drama can only benefit from acknowledging its relationship to the theatre. Neither are static. They are living forces which change and advance with every new performance and every new workshop. A great genius like Shakespeare can leap over the years and still have something of importance to say to us today – that is if we will allow his voice to be heard. We can draw thought and inspiration from all great writers, but in the right conditions we can also draw knowledge and inspiration from each other.

(B) WORKING WITH MENTALLY HANDICAPPED PEOPLE (*B. W.*)

When I first started working with mentally handicapped people I was terribly inexperienced. No one had taken the time to tell me how these people were different from 'normal' or even to point out that they *were* in some way different. As a result my early work in this area was like trying to find my way down a pitch-black passageway, with many doors leading off from it, using a small match which had constantly to be lit as I went along. The work was a series of lurches and hesitations, occasionally illuminated by the odd ray of light being shone on the subject only to be snuffed out a few seconds later. To say I had no yardsticks to work from would be an understatement and yet because I was working from scratch and by intuition I also had no preconceptions or prejudices about the people I was working with or what could be achieved.

I first started work in this area as a young adolescent. I was lucky enough to have grown up in a medical household where I was taught that all human beings have something to contribute and that human life is worth preserving at all costs. My first meetings with mentally handicapped people were based totally on my concern for the well-being of other human beings. As such I was not tainted by any clinical or statistical expectations concerning the capabilities and limitations of the people I was working with. This was an extremely valuable lesson for me, one that will stay with me all my working life. Simply put, it can be expressed as: when confronted with a human being for whom a task is supposed to be impossible, provide every opportunity for that human being to achieve the impossible.

I am now a lot older, better informed and much more experienced in working with mentally handicapped people, but I am still constantly amazed each time I begin work with a new group by the placatory and demeaning attitudes of some professionals working in this area. All too frequently mentally handicapped people are talked *at*, treated like very young children and removed from most decision-making processes – and rarely, if ever, allowed to participate in creative activities. Some of this occurs through plain ignorance. Unfortunately, some of it also occurs as a result of current training practices.

In recent years there has been a move towards the use of behaviour modification techniques in the training of mentally handicapped adolescents and adults with this move being particularly strong in the USA and Canada. In some areas this 'cause and effect' approach can be very beneficial in meeting certain individuals' needs. The unfortunate side effect is that an individual's personal creativity is often suppressed or destroyed in the process. Education is reduced to an industrial assembly line so that an individual can fulfil a task in a prescribed manner with the hope being that he will be able to take on a useful role in society: usually sorting cards or putting washers in plastic bags for a pitifully poor return which in earlier times might have been described as slave wages. The behavioural approach tends to actively ignore the effective domain and in some cases seeks to deliberately atrophy it because innovation and personal expression can impede the development of task-orientated behavioural goals. This is the background that the drama specialist works in and against in her interactions with mentally handicapped adolescents, adults and to a lesser extent children.

The problems presented by people suffering from mental handicaps are often not simply those of the handicapping condition but are to a large extent the responsibility of the societies in which they live. Modern industrial societies tend to pursue a policy of exclusion and whilst times are slowly changing this sheltering of mentally handicapped people from the pressures of life, however well-meaning, tends to compound their problems. In effectively segregating mentally handicapped people from the rest of society they are made even more of an enigma for people with whom their contact is, at best, minimal. As a result of an unfamiliarity with human beings coat-hanger terms such as 'mentally handicapped' abound as do the many misconceptions concerning them. In such a short space I cannot redress the injustices that societies perpetrate on their special populations. Nor can I convey the uniqueness of Peter or Susan, George or Mary or all the other mentally handicapped people I have worked with – each was special, needing to be met and understood, not simply distilled into a few sentences. However, I will attempt to make a few simple observations in the hope that others will not be swayed by social stereotypes. At the same time I hope to provide some pointers regarding some of the approaches to drama with mentally handicapped people but not so many that I produce preconceptions in the reader as to *the* way of working.

Mentally handicapped people, to greater or lesser degrees, suffer some form of developmental delay. This delay impedes the completion of one or more tasks which we would normally take for granted. Different people find different tasks taxing but each task will present that mentally handicapped person with a greater problem for its successful completion than would normally have been expected from the average individual at the same stage of development. This might mean that the task takes longer than average to complete or in some cases make it impossible for that individual to complete it at all. At the risk of oversimplifying, developmental delays mean that tasks take longer to learn, are more difficult to remember and present the individual with difficulty in transferring knowledge learnt at one task to another. As a result each task may have to be started from scratch each time.

It is very important to be aware that not all tasks are affected uniformly. In fact many mentally handicapped people show 'islands of brilliance' where activities are undertaken and completed at a much higher level than might have been expected solely on observation and assessment of previous work. This is particularly true in creative areas such as Social Drama. Frequently, people with mental handicaps surpass expectations while participating in drama sessions, sometimes amazing professionals who have worked with them for years. There could be a number of reasons why this happens. One is that few, if any, assessment tests are designed to measure personal creativity. This is not particularly surprising for creativity is such a difficult quality to define, let alone assess. Perhaps even more importantly the arts (dance, drama, music, visual art) have the power to stir the imagination and engage the emotions in a way that perhaps no other activities can. Through enjoyment, imaginative stimulus and emotional release they can motivate individuals to surpass expected achievements. In dramatic activity mentally handicapped people can be themselves and make use of their creative potential. Under the guidance of a skilled leader they can be encouraged to make use of their imaginations, engage their emotions and as a result participate in and complete tasks that are 'beyond them'.

In enabling these people to participate in drama, rather than being passive spectators, the drama specialist may put himself at variance with other professionals working with the same group. It is important that specialists are aware that by involving people actively in drama they may make themselves unpopular. However, it is equally important not to shirk from a responsibility to allow mentally handicapped people the chance to participate in and grow from dramatic activities.

No two mentally handicapped people are exactly alike. They come in all shapes and sizes, there is no 'prototype' mentally handicapped person and whilst certain specific conditions produce some similarity of physical characteristics (e.g. Down's Syndrome), each individual is unique. Contrary to popular opinion, mentally handicapped people are not always happy and obliging. As with everyone else individuals show a full range of emotions and moods. These are affected by external influences such as professionals attempting to reduce the level and number of 'unacceptable' behaviours – with the unacceptability being decided by the professional, not the individual exhibiting them.

People with mental handicaps are not mentally ill; however, there may often be secondary emotional disorders which occur as a result of social pressures, frustration, difficulties posed by communication and an inability to make themselves understood. These emotional disorders are often context-specific, possibly produced or compounded by the insensitivity of some of the professionals with whom they come into contact. Sometimes, these disorders abate or totally disappear when the person is actively involved in creative pursuits.

Points to remember

The uniqueness of individuals with developmental delays and emotional 'flexibility' make it nearly impossible to plan for that nebulous group known as '*the* mentally handicapped'. However, there are some basic ideas which may be helpful in preparing a Social Drama session for your group with all their hopes, fears, loves and hates.

- In general all the basic rules outlined in Chapter 3 apply to working with groups of mentally handicapped people.
- Probably the most important facet of the session is in the presentation of your material. This presentation will require you to do your homework about your group. It is very important that you make yourself familiar with the language capabilities of your group, as communication of your materials is essential to the success of a session. Choose your words carefully. Use language that is appropriate to the level of understanding of your group. However, don't simply reinforce the current language level but always attempt to stretch your group. This may be made easier for you if you are working with a mixed-ability group. Present and explain the games and activities in more than one way and always reinforce with gestural clues. In many cases it may be beneficial to model the activity (i.e. do a 'dry run' before asking your group to participate in the activity).
- Always allow ample time for the group to familiarize themselves with each activity. Try and break the activities down into simple sections and progress step by step, always building on the previous stage.
- Wherever appropriate engage in conversation with your group before, during and after each activity or game. This

communication provides you with essential feed-back and allows the group to feel part of the decision-making process. Obviously activities which require quiet and sensitivity do not lend themselves to discussion whilst they are in progress.

– Don't be fooled by professional reports that tell you that 'John is aggressive', or that 'Michael has no imagination', as these general comments must be placed in context. Michael may have a fabulous imagination but has never been given the opportunity where he feels safe to use it and John may be aggressive only because he is angry at not being allowed to express himself. I have found mentally handicapped people to be just as creative as anyone else; they just need time and a safe place to allow their creativity to see the light of day. In fact their honest 'sense of reality' is often a refreshing change from the guarded and jaded response we have come to expect from our daily interactions in this fast-paced world.

– The dramatic process, emphasizing as it does the healthy development of unique personal expression, may place the drama specialist in conflict with the behavioural objectives professional colleagues hold for the same client. In many ways this makes it all the more important that the drama specialist pursues the dramatic process as a means for the client's right to individual personal expression. However, this requires a high degree of tact and diplomacy, particularly with senior professional colleagues, if there is to be any chance of success. For in order that Social Drama, Drama or Drama Therapy sessions may be offered to mentally handicapped people it is essential that you articulate and, wherever possible, demonstrate to colleagues the benefits such programmes hold for the groups you work with. This will often necessitate proving that a drama programme complements and enhances the work pursued in other programme approaches. This may present either moral or aesthetic dilemmas for the fledgling and experienced drama specialist alike; but, these problems must be faced and overcome if the work is to continue to flourish and succeed.

(C) WORKING WITH PHYSICALLY HANDICAPPED PEOPLE (B. W.)

As with many complex areas encountered peripherally in everyday life, there is a tendency for most people to reduce physical conditions to convenient shorthand labels. This obviously helps in day-to-day conversation, speeds comprehension and enables people to nod their heads in agreement. However, it does nothing to convey the enormous range and depth of disabling conditions covered by the euphemism 'physical handicap'. In a sense while this shorthand label is a convenient way of acknowledging a rudimentary understanding, it can also act as a barrier to delving deeper and discovering many of the complexities presented by specific physical handicaps. The first task of the drama specialist is to look beyond these barriers.

Physical handicaps can occur at any state of a person's life. The disabling condition can occur at birth; through a genetic aberration; as a result of a birth trauma or due to a surgical complication related to delivery. A physical handicap can occur later in life; through the delayed action of a genetic aberration, as a result of accidental injury or through an environmental disaster. As we approach our senior years the general wear and tear of everyday bodily functions slowly start taking their toll eventually causing the body to slow down or, in some cases, even break down. This too can result in various forms of physical handicaps.

No one is exempt. Physical handicaps ignore barriers of sex, creed and colour. They cut across socio-economic and class boundaries. Anybody can be disabled by a physical handicap. Some conditions may be temporary, such as a broken arm, causing a minor inconvenience and a period of reduced capabilities in dealing with the daily environment. Other conditions remain permanent continuing to affect the way individuals cope with their environment for the rest of their lives. Some physical conditions noticeably affect the quality of an individual's life and a few reduce an individual's life expectancy – occasionally quite drastically. No matter what the type or severity of the physical limitation, drama can have a valuable role to play in enriching that person's life and personal growth.

The drama specialist is always faced with a problem concerning the planning of sessions for each individual's capabilities. As I have said, there is a tendency to view problems in terms of labels or categories. However, there is always a need to plan for each drama session on the basis of the needs and abilities of that particular group. Often the specialist does not have time to plan for each individual medical condition but must still be alert to the physical limitations being faced by the individuals in the group. *Initially*, the root cause of the physical problem is, to an extent, less important than the restrictions it imposes on that individual. I am not in any way suggesting that knowledge of the root cause of limitation (e.g. a restriction of locomotion), is not important; however, in the initial stages a drama specialist has to deal with providing experiences which meet the *physical* needs of the individuals. The fact that the restriction is known to have been caused by family violence or through spina bifida is obviously essential for the development of later, deeper work. However, this information, relating to the cause of the physical limitation, will have to wait until a rapport has been built between the drama specialist and the group, before it can be used to full effect.

In working with physically handicapped people the drama specialist may come into contact with a wide range of physical disorders. It is unrealistic to expect that she will be familiar with the psychological implications and aetiology of all the physical conditions that might be encountered; but a working knowledge of the disorders affecting the individuals in her group is essential.[3] There are two major areas of concern which she should be particularly conscious of when working with physically handicapped individuals, namely: how does the specific disabling condition affect the individuals' interactions with their environment; and, what stigmas are attached to the physical condition?

In dealing with the effect of physical conditions on these interactions, the specialist should, I believe, consider three major groups of restrictions:

- *Sensory Impairments* – Physical conditions that result in the partial or complete loss of one or more sense, of which loss of hearing or of sight are the most commonly encountered.

- *Restricted Mobility* – Mobility restrictions can be related to *locomotion* or to *gesture*. Locomotion deals with movement of the whole body while gesture refers to movement of any of the limbs or body parts (e.g. arms, head, hands).

- *Multiple Handicaps* – This might be a combination of the

previous groups; a combination of one of the above with another handi-capping condition (e.g. epilepsy or diabetes); or a combination of a physical and a mental handicap.

The physical condition and the restrictions it imposes are not the only problem facing the drama specialist. Often a far more difficult problem she must prepare for relates to the stigmas attached to the physical condition. These stigmas can be of two kinds: those placed on the condition by the individuals suffering from it (i.e. the mental attitude of the sufferer towards his disabling condition); and those attributed to the condition by the society in which the sufferer has to survive (i.e. the limitations projected on to the condition by those members of society *not* suffering from it). These personal and social stigmas have possibly more bearing on the way an individual copes with day-to-day living than the physical condition itself.

The society in which the disabled person lives creates an initial framework in which he responds to his physical restrictions; for his attitude to restricted mobility or sensory impairment is based on the social stigma attached to it by that society. The response of the non-handicapped members of his own community, stereotypes (to an extent) his initial responses to his physical condition. The disabled person is at the mercy of the whims and fads of society. At one moment he may be excluded from society and locked in a home, 'for his own protection'; at another he may be a freak, on show for the benefit of society; while at others he may be a normal human being who simply has more difficulty crossing a busy street than most.

The disabled person can either reinforce or reject these stereotypes, and each person has the ability to choose either way. My late friend Dennis, disabled since birth and confined to a wheelchair for the last part of his life, made a conscious decision to reject society's stereotyping of chair-bound individuals as being mentally handicapped. As Dennis often said, 'I may be confined to this chair but I'm not stupid.' Or as my wife Roberta often says, 'I may have a disability but I'm not going to give up living life to the full.' Roberta once referred to Dennis as 'a long-distance runner' because despite always having to battle uphill to achieve his goals, he never gave up hope. Right up to the point when his life was so tragically cut short by cancer, he believed that his career as an actor and film director was about to take off.

Dennis' handicap was visible. It enabled society to pinpoint him as a disabled person. It made many day-to-day tasks difficult, some impossible without assistance, but his positive perception of himself was an example, an education, to other disabled people and to the society in which he lived. Much of this positive self-attitude, the lack of stigma he attached to his disability, was (as Dennis was the first to admit) a direct result of his involvement with drama, dance and art.

Not everyone is like Dennis or Roberta. Many people become bitter and almost give up living. They not only accept the social stereotyping of their condition but they amplify the process of stigmatization. A young man I know contracted Multiple Sclerosis in his early twenties. His response was to wallow in self-pity and be angry at the world and the hand that fate had dealt him. It is true that in his case he was treated particularly unfairly by his employer, but his response over subsequent years has been to reinforce the negative perceptions some members of society have of disabled people as a group.

Social Drama, by enabling disabled people to achieve success in their personal interactions within a 'safe' environment, can help them to build a positive self-image. No matter how different individuals' disabling conditions are, our general approach to people should remain the same. For in the early stages of our work we must focus on what the individual *can* do! We should attempt to select exercises that emphasize *strengths* not *weaknesses* (e.g. for the visually impaired person using activities which emphasize tactile or aural sensations). Later on we may wish to introduce games and exercises which enable the individual to face and discuss the limitations and perceptions of their specific conditions. However, this stage can only be approached once an atmosphere of trust and a belief in the dramatic process, and the drama specialist facilitating it, have been established. Even then there is a strong chance that the very act of bringing discussion of the condition into the open may create a flood of mixed feelings and emotions. The discussion of a physical handicap may be very traumatic and can, if incorrectly handled, result in emotional regression. Remember the great need for care and sensitivity when using drama with physically handicapped people.

Points to remember

In working with physically handicapped people there are a number of factors to consider over and above the general preparations outlined in Chapter 3.

- The diversity and severity of physical limitations presented by each individual are essential pieces of information for planning the session.
- Plan for the *physical* needs of your group initially.
- Plan for mixed ability groups, as opposed to groups of similar disabilities. This requires greater forethought but often allows for greater opportunities for personal growth

and development for those involved.

- Try to get the group to work together. Teaming an individual in a wheelchair with a person with a visual impairment can help to 'cancel out' their individual physical limitations. This sharing of strengths and abilities is as important in groups who are brought together through a common denominator (e.g. spina bifida or epilepsy) as it is for a more 'mixed' group, for it enables the group to gain first-hand experience of working together to overcome physical limitations. It also enables them to see that everyone is an individual and not just 'physically handicapped'. This is an important change that must occur in both individual and social perceptions of disabling conditions if there is to be any chance of overcoming the stigmas which prevent disabled people from participating fully in society.

- As always names are important. Never forget that physically handicapped individuals are people and that some very important figures in the historical development of culture and human thought were themselves physically disabled (e.g. Roosevelt, Beethoven, Matisse, Paganini, Christy Brown, and so the list goes on).

- Choose language appropriate to the age and life experiences of the group. At all costs avoid 'talking down' to the group.

- Physically handicapped people are not mentally handicapped or emotionally disturbed; however, some mentally handicapped people have additional physical handicaps, and people with physical limitations may exhibit an emotional disturbance (this may or may not be directly attributable to the specific physical problem).

- Plan for the strengths and capabilities of your group (i.e.

plan for sensory impairments, mobility restrictions or multiple handicaps in a way that emphasizes individual strengths).

- Start from where the group is – if the people have severe limitations to their mobility, either confined to wheelchairs or forced to use ambulatory aids, then plan for chair-based activities initially.
- Attempt to emphasize imaginative skills that overcome physical limitations and enable participants to make use of the 'props' that come with their physical limitations.
- If you do work with a group solely comprised of people with physical disabilities always work towards enabling the participants to take part in integrated drama workshops.
- Aim to make yourself redundant. In certain economic climates this is not difficult! However, a leader can make herself redundant through her skill in enabling the members of her group to re-integrate in society and *not* because some politician decrees it from on high.

(D) WORKING WITH EMOTIONALLY DISTURBED PEOPLE (R. W.)

We all have emotions, and at some times in our lives they become disturbed. The degree to which such disturbances affect our behaviour, and how much help we need to cope with the problem depends on all sorts of factors. We may recover quickly or gradually or we may carry an emotional burden for life. Those of us who work with emotionally disturbed people recognize the diversity of problems that our groups are having to face, and it is our job to help the individuals to tackle their difficulties on their own terms; to use their own strengths to bring about their own recovery.

I have just completed three years' work at a residential community for emotionally disturbed adolescents. Partly because I know this environment well, and partly because adolescents often exemplify and exaggerate the problems of the wider category, I would like to talk mostly about my work with this community before drawing some wider conclusions about using Social Drama with emotionally disturbed people.

I can still remember my first session with the boys at that home (it was not a mixed community when I started there). In a cavernous, dimly lit, converted Methodist chapel I stood waiting. Eight youngsters stormed in and started swinging from the beams, disappearing out of the other doors, pulling the curtains down and generally making the Methodist ghosts flee into the streets. Trying to start from basics I said, 'O.K., let's get into a circle.' They didn't! It had never happened to me before, at least not on my own. There was no one there to back me up or suggest another idea. Eventually, more through boredom than anything, they accepted that getting into a circle wasn't too much to ask and we played a simple name game. I survived the session by playing 'Chair Swap' (see game 10) with them for over an hour until the van came. I collapsed in an exhausted and disillusioned heap. I could not do my job, it seemed, and I would do as well to pack my bags and go back where I came from. Fortunately something made me stay and try again. The next day saw a different (and wilder) group bundle into the hall. 'Are we going to do that immature game?' they asked, already sitting in a circle of chairs. 'If you want to,' I said and they played it for ten minutes. 'Do you know any others?' My diary lists nine things we did that afternoon, only one of which failed to go down well. I was now more of a known quantity and the other group had obviously spoken to this one who now knew that Social

Drama was 'all right' or even 'a laugh'. They had been reassured (but not in so many words) that Social Drama was non-threatening and apparently nothing to do with the fact that they had 'problems'. Social Drama never looked back and I occasionally meet boys from those early days who want to know if I still do such silly things and whether I remember the time when . . .

I continued to believe in Social Drama as a force in these people's lives. I knew that many of them had seen more of the world's iniquity in thirteen years than I would in thirty. More importantly, many of them did not consider their experiences unusual. After all, they had never had a different sort of childhood, and many of the children they were living with had similar tales to tell. One of the most notable effects of this premature thrust into adulthood was their prevalent *im*maturity in dealing with everyday problems. Another was that their notions of 'care' and 'play' (so central to Social Drama) had become twisted by their predicament and the system in which they were trapped. They were 'in care', 'on a Care Order' and under the strict supervision of 'care staff'. Care was something that was done to you. It was something that happened to you if your family broke up. It was something that you were punished with if you shoplifted or skived off school. Meanwhile, in the playground, there was very little creative play. The youngsters stood around moping, jostling, fighting, teasing and shouting. They competed at pool and Space Invaders, but rarely did I see them 'lifted' by their playing. What genuinely playful activity I saw was usually with a member of staff, and it became apparent that this was often the basis of a relationship between adults and children. One 11-year-old (considered to be amongst the most disruptive) would constantly steal his teacher's keys as a joke. It was a way of relating to the adult wherein the boy was in charge. When I started to get to know him better he began to steal my keys. Such relationships are very common in all sorts of institutions and it is very easy for either party to maintain them at a superficial level and never to develop them. I wanted to explore the potential of this sort of relationship in the Social Drama setting.

At the same time I was interested in one particular unit which was encouraged to work in a slightly different way. It was 'home' for 18 younger, less mature, more emotional boys and was staffed by people more sympathetic to what I was trying to do. I spent some off-duty time in the unit, eating there, watching T.V., playing darts, going to the shops, anything which would help us to get to know one another. I wasn't a member of staff to them at these times, more of a visitor. I began to notice a change in the attitude of these boys when they were in my Social Drama groups. They were less likely to be disruptive, more involved, more willing to trust me. As one of the staff from that unit explained, 'My job is to redress imbalances in these children's lives. I do it by establishing a relationship with each child (which I want both of us to value) and then I use that relationship to help him manipulate his own recovery. You are doing the same.' I have paraphrased him slightly, but that is the essence of his explanation, and it is one that I have continued to explore ever since.

By having a relationship with the children which extended outside the Social Drama workshops, the work that we did in that old chapel began to have a wider significance. And, very importantly, there was not always any need to verbalize this significance. There is a tendency to believe that insight is the most powerful tool you can give someone to help them recover from emotional difficulties. Social Drama does not always work in this way and is quite prepared to use metaphor, unspoken feelings and allusions to help people to grow. It has much more to do with intuition than interpretation; it is more 'feelingful' than 'meaningful'. People at risk can easily grow tired of being 'treated', being 'made better', discussing their progress and charting their improvements. This is especially true for emotionally disturbed people who often do not (or will not) recognize that there is anything unusual or treatable about their condition. This is why Social Drama can be so valuable: it is not offered as a treatment and it is not stigmatic to attend the sessions. It is therapeutic, because it is concerned with growth and development, but that does not mean that it has to be presented or received as treatment.

After about six months at the children's community the foundation stones of Social Drama were laid. Then, partly as an aid to discipline, partly to broaden the scope of the workshops and partly to get Social Drama accepted in a wider field, I began to invite students from a local college into the sessions. It had many advantages. The youngsters mixed with, played with, worked with and grew with people they would not otherwise have met. They formed valuable ties with them and often met them outside of sessions. They saw that other people were prepared to play these games, enjoy them and appreciate them. The feeling that Social Drama was for anybody who wanted it became more widespread. We got more and better work done than ever before and students, visitors and outsiders have been a regular component of the work ever since. It is a genuinely important option to consider expanding a Social Drama group because, as we have said elsewhere, it is an ascriptive activity for all, not a prescriptive treatment for the few.

I have talked so far about work in a residential setting for emotionally disturbed adolescents but most of these points hold true for working outside institutions and with other age groups.

Always the base is that Social Drama helps people by enabling them to explore small portions of human experience in a safe but challenging environment. It follows that we, as leaders must create a safely challenging relationship with our groups and that the sessions must constitute a comforting opportunity to discover, grow and celebrate.

An atmosphere of mutual trust is important in all groups, but particularly when you are working with emotionally disturbed people. The use of trust games in this respect is vital but it is not enough on its own. They must be incorporated into your efforts to build an emotionally stable base for you and your group to work from. In the early stages you may find that you do not play many games or have much discussion. It is even worth considering avoiding identifiable sessions to begin with and just meeting your group members in a different setting – the canteen, the lounge, at an informal gathering or even on an outing. In these cases you can present yourself as someone who 'would like to do some work with you if you are interested'. If they have taken to you as an individual you may already have aroused their curiosity, and at least you will not be strangers to each other at the first workshop.

In the early days you must tread carefully and not ask too much of your group. Social Drama touches emotions, and until you have had the chance to watch your clients in action you will not be entirely sure in which areas they are vulnerable and responsive. You must keep close contacts with other professionals who know your group, for they will give you some indications, but there is no substitute for first-hand observation. Choose games with which you are completely confident and which do not demand too much of the players. Be prepared to alter the games to suit the group's abilities and moods, and give constant encouragement and reassurance to those who seem to need it. Observe and respond. In this way you will begin to form a foundation for your later work.

It is a good idea to join in as many activities as possible at the start, as this encourages involvement and helps the group members to trust you more. But when you reach deeper levels it may be important for you to stand on the sidelines. You can observe more from there and your group may become uneasy if they see you revealing too much of your inner self. The session is for their benefit more than yours.

Every workshop involves a new beginning and you must assess the emotional mood and needs of the group each time it assembles. Don't start straight away but take time to talk with people about what they have been doing since you last saw them. Be prepared to change your workshop-plan to cope with what you find. When you do start remember to reaffirm the security of the setting in some way. Play a favourite game, perhaps, develop an opening ritual with the group or simply ask them how *they* would like to begin. I have sometimes asked a group to place themselves *exactly* as they were at the end of the previous session. This creates a sense of continuity and can encourage people to reflect on their state of mind and the sort of work you are doing together. Remember that you will be unlikely to get very far until people are relaxed, comfortable and unafraid.

The practical problems of using Social Drama with this sort of group determine and are determined by the games you choose to play. I have already mentioned the time when I could not get a group to form a circle (a common problem) and there is often a strong sense of suspicion when you try and introduce something unusual. Hopefully you will develop some of the necessary trust for your group to follow you into new experiences but you can help this along by 'sandwiching' new and challenging games between tried and accepted ones. Alternatively, you can play a popular game and then vary it slightly to make it more demanding or open-ended. Your group should become progressively happier with this sort of development.

Among the most valuable experiences you can encourage with emotionally disturbed people are trust exercises, physical and eye-contact games, communication games and (eventually) discussion. Of course, these are the ones which some people (usually the ones who may benefit most) will try to avoid. Don't be unduly worried by this; take your time, use trust, be reassuring, use what readiness there is from others within the group to explore these activities and let the reticent watch what happens. When they see that things are safe, as well as challenging, they may be prepared to try the experience themselves. In the meantime, try to accept that watching may be as valuable for them as participating (it often is for everyone).

Most groups of emotionally disturbed people are heterogeneous. You will consequently have different demands and expectations placed on you by different members of the group. While one member may need to play very simple, undemanding games, another may view them as unnecessary or demeaning. You might wish to explore this in terms of what we do 'need' or what really is 'good for us', but more often you should be looking for material and a style of working which can cater for as much of the capability spectrum as possible. It is not hard to find or invent more demanding roles within a game for those that can cope. And asking a more able member to help a less confident one can sometimes provide both of them with the sort of interaction they need to practise. Caring works in two directions and we must not see our clients purely as *recipients* of concern.

Most specialists who have worked with emotionally disturbed people will tell you of the discipline problems involved. The group members are frequently disruptive, abusive, aggressive, poorly motivated and unresponsive. It is easy to think 'I could get so much more done if they would just shut up and listen', but getting them to shut up and listen is *part* of what has to be done. (To take such an attitude would be like working with a group of physically handicapped people and wishing they were all able to walk and run so that you could do more movement workshops with them.) A group of compliant, unquestioning sheep would offer you many fewer problems, but would you need to work with them? We don't want discipline problems in our groups but they come with the job and they must, first and foremost, be dealt with inside the group. Ideally attendance at Social Drama should be completely optional, though I recognize this is not always the case. The most important thing a group can give a leader is their consent, for only then will you be able to begin work. If you are in the unfortunate position of having 'conscripts' in your group then you can give them the option of sitting out. It may be important for them to take that option for reasons that you (and possibly they) cannot understand. They may not do as much this way, but at least when they do get involved it will be because they choose to.

Be ready to use the session itself as the discipline. After all, we are trying to help people respond on their own behalf to the pressures and circumstances of the world. One of your first problems may simply be to keep the group in the room. Use a game like Prisoners (see game 8) or more indirectly Break Out (see game 66) as a way of handling or alluding to the problem. Use some of the other games in Section IV that are indicated as helping to channel aggression. More importantly, make your sessions so attractive that no one wants to leave. The peer group often holds the best card, for it is harder for someone to disrupt his enthusiastic peers than his overworked and nervous leader.

Remember also that group members may disrupt a session for reasons other than malice. It may be that they feel too challenged, nervous or upset about what the group process is doing to them or that they cannot handle too much freedom. They will not be able to tell you this, but you must learn to recognize the signs. You must develop a sensitive understanding of how far to take your group and how fast to travel. It is easy to stay at a very superficial level in your relationships with the group and the sort of things you explore with them. It is equally easy to uncover a highly vulnerable part of somebody's history or feelings. If you are not prepared or able to deal with this *there and then* you may do more harm than good. Social Drama will expose raw nerve endings and you must be careful never to work at a level beyond your capabilities or the needs and wishes of your group.

Points to remember

The more general points on preparation and planning outlined in Chapter 3 apply, but it is particularly important to note:

- Start from where you are. You must work from a point which is emotionally stable for you and for your group. You are working with people who are steeped in insecurity and doubt, and you must offer them a safe foundation on which to build their recovery.
- Remember that every session involves a new beginning and that you must not assume anything about the emotional state of any individual. Favourite games, simple rituals and name games are good starters which reaffirm everyone's

security.

- Try never to work too far or too fast. You are trying to help people achieve their recovery at their own pace, and if you lead them too quickly you may do more harm than good.
- Recognize the type of relationship that you have with the group and its members. Be prepared to use these relationships as a way of extending the relevance of the workshops – otherwise it can be easy for people to think that caring, warmth and sensitivity are only important in the Social Drama workshop and not outside it.
- Try not to let the group get stuck with operating at a superficial level. When they are confident and ready you can lead them in to a deeper understanding of the work you are doing with them.
- Be prepared to work covertly, offering feelings as well as insight. Work through metaphor and allusion as much as direct explanation.
- Trust games and games of physical contact are particularly valuable with emotionally disturbed people. You must, however, create a climate where these activities are not just done for their own sake but reinforce an existing atmosphere of confidence and challenge.
- Accept that you are likely to have discipline problems and that that is partly why you are there. Deal with them within the sessions wherever possible.
- Keep good contacts with other professionals who work with your group so that you can tell each other of any important developments. Try also to ask your group members what they are doing the rest of the week and be prepared to use this information within the workshop.
- Consider opening the sessions to other people as part of a

policy of removing the idea that 'you are here for treatment' and replacing it with 'we are here for Social Drama'.

(E) WORKING WITH SENIORS (B. W.)

Seniors[4] as a group, experience many of the problems already discussed under other headings in this chapter. Whilst we have discussed the basic problems of physical limitations and mental frailties; the problems faced by the senior, particularly the institutionalized senior, are somewhat different in nature.

The problems all individuals eventually experience are directly attributable to the general wear and tear of the body; the mechanical breakdown which we are all slowly experiencing and which accelerates, to different degrees, as we approach the twilight of our days. The problems faced by seniors are ones of ageing; however, failing faculties and continuing physical degeneration cause different reactions in different individuals. Some are able to accept the changes easily, seeing them as part of life's rich tapestry. Others continue to deny the changes, exercising and extending themselves in an attempt to combat them. Still others become bitter and angry at the world and the lot that has befallen them; whilst a few withdraw into a cocoon preparing for the death that they believe to be both near and inevitable. These are but a sample of the responses encountered and show the wide range of attitudes engendered by the physical changes that advancing years can bring.

In addition to physical changes there may also be changes in cognitive functioning. As people get older there is a tendency towards forgetfulness, slower speech, loss of concentration and momentary loss of contact with the present. These lapses, or reflections on the past, are neither particularly unhealthy or uncommon. However, some individuals may suffer acute psychological changes (e.g. regression to child-like state, personality change, severe mood-swings etc.) and these may be accentuated by the changes in the pattern of life and the problems these pose for day-to-day living.

At different times cultures have dealt with the seniors in their midst in different and often ingenious ways. In our western technological societies, seniors are often viewed as having reached a point where they can no longer be of service to the rest of the society. The senior is then forced to retire, at a fixed age because society deems they can no longer be of use to the workforce. This often leaves individuals with a sense of worthlessness. Having been productive all their working lives they now have to find ways to fill their time. One individual I know (having been in public service which required him to wake at 7 a.m. and be out before 8 a.m.) spent the first few years of retirement keeping to his work schedule, and was out working in his garden or garage because he didn't want the neighbours to think he was lazy. This man, like so many who are forced to retire, still had many years of service and a wealth of stored knowledge to bring to his job.[5]

In the natural scheme of things the problems of advancing years will have to be faced by all of us. The advances in medical science, coupled with our increased awareness of the role that diet plays in avoiding many of the major life-shortening diseases, mean that people are living longer. As a person gets older this may cause problems for the family, who for one reason or another choose to place this senior member of the family into a residential home. Unfortunately, many of these homes strive to remove the last vestiges of human dignity from their residents. They strip them of possessions, of privacy and often of their will to survive and replace these with an institutionalised ritual and physical dependence on the professional staff in the home. As an example: a couple, who happened to be two of Western Canada's most famous artists, had to give up their house, studio and personal belongings. They were placed in a nursing home which compelled them to give up the only precious thing they had left – each other. After over 50 years of marriage the nursing home commanded them to sleep in separate rooms and to share those rooms with another person of their own sex. The possessions, which said something about their personalities were removed and their pets were destroyed.[6] Everything is designed to change independent adults into dependent children, from the moment they walk in the front door to the day they are carried out.

Seniors are far from being useless members of society. They have a very important role to play in family structures and society as a whole, as keepers of the family's heritage and guardians of the oral tradition. Traditionally wisdom and knowledge are conveyed orally. In recent times with the emergence of printing presses, books, a literate population and more recently the influence of television, the emphasis on oral communication has diminished. Nevertheless, whilst more and more wisdom is being conveyed through books and electronic mouthpieces, people are still the vessels by which that wisdom is channelled. For, whilst wisdom is not directly correlated to age, it is very closely linked to experience. As a result seniors often have fascinating stories to tell about their lives: how jobs used to be carried out; the hardships of different eras and so on. Whilst some older people may have no formal education to speak of they will all have experienced life.

Seniors have the capacity to offer highly informed comment on cultural change, social evolution and family history. They have a wealth of information to share and the drama leader can often gain fascinating insights on the place in which her group is working and living. I was leading a session with a group of seniors in Alberta. It transpired that one man was born and bred in the area. Not only that, but at one time he had owned one of the biggest cattle ranches in the area that had now become Calgary. In fact he had sold his farm to the Calgary city council, who had designated it as development land and on which now stood the house that my family and I were living in. This man was a walking encyclopaedia of local history with some fascinating tales which would have brightened up any school's History or Social Science classes.

Seniors do have fascinating stories to tell, but be aware that the boundaries between fantasy and reality may sometimes become a little fuzzy. For some this difference may be easily distinguished and only become muddled for reasons of poetic license, to embellish their story; for others the distinction is not so easily made. Sometimes, fantasy and reality cannot be distinguished or separated, occasionally to the extent that all concepts of time and place are lost, they are permanently 'living somewhere else'.

Points to remember

In working with seniors there are some factors that should be borne in mind over and above the points covered in Chapter 3.
- Seniors may be slow to become actively involved. Occasionally this may produce a 'wall of inertia' that has to be scaled prior to the start of each session.
- Some people will simply want to sit in their chair. (This should be interpreted literally!) Individuals often count a particular chair as their possession and woe betide the ignorant drama leader who sits in it by mistake.

- Many will see what you do as 'kids's stuff'. It is very difficult to introduce Social Drama activities to seniors who have always lived their life by the 'Protestant work ethic'. They think that play is for children and that games are played competitively or not at all.
- Some people will be over-anxious to participate. These over-willing volunteers need to be encouraged but not allowed to overshadow quieter members of the group or (more importantly) prevent the hesitant from joining in.
- Be prepared to work slowly. Activities will probably be interspersed with general discussion. In many cases the talking is as important, if not more important, than the activities.
- Start to develop a 'listener's ear' – it is important to be able to pick up on the concerns of the members of the group.
- Employ activities that emphasize the group's strengths (e.g. story-telling games, particularly those that allow individuals to dramatize personal tales).
- Use language that is appropriate to the group; all too often seniors are talked to as though they are children, this is terribly demeaning.
- Try to choose games that will extend the group and get them moving. Start with chair-based movement games and then provide a reason for people to move out of their chairs. Too much of a senior's life is decided by other people without any reference to the individual's feelings. Activities that genuinely make them want to get up off their chair to dance or sing or act are essential to the development of the sessions.
- Many seniors in homes spend their lives isolated from human touch. The need to be hugged or touched can be very strong but it can also be very frightening! Select

activities which allow for human contact in a non-threatening way.

- Avoid reinforcing physical dependency. Wherever possible encourage the individual to do tasks for themselves with the minimum of external help.
- Make use of Social Drama activities wherever and whenever they seem appropriate. Betty O'Brien started her work with a group of seniors who were always lined up for a meal (anything up to an hour prior to the meal being served). Betty filled this otherwise vacant hour, the people simply sitting waiting, with beneficial and enjoyable drama activities.
- Be prepared for members of your group to stop coming. This may be temporary because of illness or a doctor's appointment but it may be permanent. It is sometimes a shock to the person working with seniors when members of the group die but it is something that has to be expected and it doesn't mean a leader cannot grieve for the loss of a friend.
- Try to remain humble. The people you work with are often far more knowledgeable than you are. They have a wealth of information, ideas and feelings to share with you if you let them. It is always a sobering thought, but remind yourself that there is a strong chance that you will end up in the same situation as the members of your group. Always treat them as you would wish to be treated yourself.

Notes

A. *Educational Drama*

1 For an explanation and theory of creative drama I refer the reader first to P. Slade, *Child Drama* (London: University of London Press, 1954).

See also the bibliography at the end of this book.

2 P. Brook, *The Empty Space* (Harmondsworth: Pelican, 1972), p. 36.

C. *Physically Handicapped People*

3 For further information, see DeLoach and Greer, *Adjustment to Severe Physical Disability: A Metamoprhosis* and Bleck and Nagel, *Physically Handicapped Children*.

E. *Seniors*

4 In this chapter we decided to use the generic term 'senior'. Many of the other popular terms (e.g. psycho-geriatric, geriatric, old men and women) carry a negative connotation and do not accept that seniors have a very positive contribution to make to their society. There is no rigid age limit involved here, though in practice the seniors one works with are generally 65 years old and often considerably older.

5 This tends to be less of a problem for women in a society which has continually confined them to the home and defined household tasks as 'women's work'. Their 'job' is not considered to be finished when they reach pensionable age. If there is any advantage at all to this invidious position it is that women who continue to be active around the home often show a slower degeneration of fine motor control.

6 This particular couple, despite the limitations being imposed on them, are still making contributions to Canadian art and literature. Young artists come and visit them and bring materials with them to work from. The administration of the home is not completely happy with this but are a little wary of removing this from their prestigious 'guests'.

SECTION III
SOCIAL DRAMA AND THE CURRICULUM

5. Towards a Therapeutic Curriculum (B.W. & R.W.)

Citizens of modern industrialized nations have come to expect a full education for themselves and their children, and in most of these countries schooling is now compulsory for children between certain ages. Adult education and vocational training are also much more widely available. This wide range of education has not always been on offer and it is interesting to examine how the structure of a society determines the type and quality of education available to the people within it. In a primitive culture people are taught what they need to know to enhance their physical, social and emotional well-being. As we might expect, more complex societies have devised intricate systems to control and transmit the increasing amounts of general and specific learning demanded by their development.[1] In this chapter we argue that the educational systems of the modern industrialized nations have often concentrated too heavily on catering for these *new* demands and have tended to neglect some of the more *basic* human needs. Social Drama, we believe, has a role to play in restoring the current imbalance.

Prior to the Industrial Revolution education was most definitely the prerogative of the privileged few. Industrialization was itself one of the major factors in the development of universal education, but the very process which acted as a catalyst in the development of an education for the poor and working classes

also mediated against their getting a good one. What industrialization did was to produce jobs which required certain skills
(numeracy, engineering, management, etc.). Education was
vocational with the skills to be taught being dictated by the needs
of the industries producing revenues for that country. Classical
education, with its emphasis on literature and the arts was, and to
a large extent still is, the luxury of the privileged few.

Since the general population first gained access to an education a little over a century ago the content of their curriculum
has been to a large extent dictated by ideologists and politicians,
who are themselves heavily influenced by the captains of
industry. Despite tremendous progress in educational thought
and some minor incursions into 'child-centred education' (a
term often misused and misunderstood) the content of educational curricula is still heavily dominated by the needs of
service and manufacturing industries. If anything this influence
has never been stronger than in our present world which is so
heavily reliant on technology and where education is continually changing to meet the ever-shifting needs of the job
market. The results have often been disastrous. Education,
rather than being a process of learning has become an industrial
production line, relentlessly reshaping reluctant pupils to meet
the dictates of the multinationals who control the job markets.[2]
There is a heavy emphasis on 'teaching', a set curriculum and,
especially in times of recession and economic hardship, a 'no-
frills' approach to educational budgeting. There seems to be an
unspoken theory that education is about teaching something
within the hallowed walls of academic establishments, for only
within those hallowed walls can an education be gained legiti-
mately. One only has to reflect on the inordinate weight given
to paper qualifications *prior* to a candidate being given an
interview to see the heavy emphasis given to formal schooling

in the job market.

People are not products. We should not go through the assembly line to be shaped into some immutable commodity that once formed stays that way forever. Human beings have the power to reason, to feel, to communicate and to change. We need continually to be stimulated or else our muscles and brain cells atrophy and eventually die.

Education has always been a life-long process of learning. This has been discussed philosophically for centuries and recently, at long last, certain 'non-traditional' post-secondary institutions have awarded credit towards degree qualifications for previous 'life experiences'. We continually need to be provided with a learning environment, one that is both stimulating and challenging, throughout our lives. This environment must not simply deal with 'objective truths', for these are temporally and culturally specific, but also with human communication and most importantly the sharing and expressing of feelings and emotions. This would necessitate a shift of emphasis from the current curriculum models with their heavy focus on skills, objectives and quantifiable end products, to a more effective, therapeutic base with an emphasis on social interaction, life experience and individual needs. This is by no means a new or unique idea though to a large extent it might still be seen as swimming against the tide, particularly by some people who influence the content of educational curricula. However, just as for the salmon returning to spawn, we feel this swimming upstream is essential to the healthy development of individuals and to the fostering of a healthy society in which we can interact.

Our lives consist of a constant succession of short plays acted out on a stage, and the success or failure of our efforts depends largely on the quality of our performance. We have to be able to script the part, as well as act it, and to make matters worse the stage and the plays are constantly changing – defined and redefined by ourselves and the other people around us. We devise and are given a series of encounters to deal with and the nature of any such encounter is affected by the context in which it occurs and by its functions. Both of these are determined to a very large extent by the participants themselves.

All social encounters take place in a context. This involves, firstly, the immediate environment: the location, the architecture, the climate, the time of day. Then there are social factors: the historical context, the cultural background and so on. The moods and feelings that the participants bring with them can obviously have an effect and this whole environment is then counterpointed and modified, in the eyes of the participants, by the roles and status of those meeting there. A tranquil park, full of the sound of mellifluous birdsong may be changed into a nightmare-world by a chance meeting with a loathed adversary and the most drab and depressing city street may suddenly be illuminated by our meeting with a loved one.

Any social exchange has a purpose. It may have been decided on in advance (e.g. an individual being interviewed for a job) or it may only become clear as the interaction takes place (e.g. a motorist being stopped for no apparent reason by a traffic policeman). The purpose of the interaction may be achieved almost instantaneously, as in a simple exchange of morning pleasantries, which once completed allows the participants to go their separate ways, or it may take an extremely long time to be completed, as in the decision to tell a lover that a relationship must end – a process which often extends long after the first meeting and purposeful interaction.

The more people who are involved in an exchange the more complicated the process of interaction becomes. Each individual brings with them their own perceptions of the scene, its context and its functions. The changing nuances of posture, gesture and inflections, are continually reflected and reshaped by the 'acting' of the other people involved, and each individual is continually re-evaluating and then reshaping their role. In order that individuals can cope with these ever-changing shifts of scene, and thus deal with the very complicated processes of normal social interaction, each of us has to be able to assess the situation quickly and carefully and then choose an appropriate role from our repertoire to meet the challenge. The ability to identify the roles demanded of us is an essential social skill without which we become conspicuous by our selecting roles which are inappropriate to the social interaction taking place.

So our success on this rapidly changing stage depends on the ability to select an appropriate role, to script it according to the context and function of the scene, to play it successfully and to improvise or even change the role abruptly to meet the changing needs. If we cannot do these things we run the risk of being seen as abnormal. Those people who are unable to cope with these demands, either through an inability to recognize them or through an inability to meet the requirements of their role (e.g. people with mental handicaps) can easily be identified as being different. Their difference may be seen as a harmless idiosyncrasy, such as a comic affectation or flamboyant expression, or it may be perceived as something sinister or dangerous to other members of the society and result in the individual being subjected to treatment for their 'disorder'. However, it is important to recognize that the 'disorder' is defined not by the individual exhibiting it but by the society with whom he interacts. Socially acceptable behaviour is always culturally defined. We have known individuals who have been institutionalized for the best part of their lives and whose only 'disorder' was to have been born out of wedlock, or to have been born blind, or simply to have been homeless. Some of these individuals have spent more than 50 years locked away, being treated for a condition deemed socially inappropriate all those years before. Once in the institution, of course, their behaviour becomes more conditioned and is used to justify their continued 'treatment'.

Recognizing and adjusting to the many social stages we encounter in our day-to-day interactions are essential and mostly subconscious skills needed for healthy, normal and inconspicuous operation. Those people who find these skills difficult will be identified as failures and often deemed to be in need of treatment. This often takes the form of remodelling their socially inappropriate role behaviours so that they may once again take their place with the rest of society. But to a large extent it is society's and not the 'socially inept' individual's fault that these daily interactions cause so much of a problem. In particular the current concept of education, with its heavy emphasis on schooling, does little to alleviate or address the problems posed by social interactions.

What we are arguing is a return to the absolute basics of education, not those supposed basics imposed by pragmatists during times of economic restraint, but the real basics of education, namely the human interaction between individuals within a learning environment. In the short-term this would be a difficult and costly procedure but in the long-term we feel sure this would prove 'cost effective' as many of the individuals who currently require expensive treatment and restraint (through psychiatric counselling, probation, prison, etc.) would be better equipped to deal with those daily social roles which currently set them apart from the rest of the society in which they live and eventually place them in need of 'treatment'.

This is not going to happen overnight, nor are the powers that shape societies likely to relinquish their stranglehold on the social economics which so shape industrialized societies' ways of thought and action. However, we believe, in common with many notable artists, educators and arts therapists, that the arts have a prominent part to play in all aspects of human development and this becomes even more acutely obvious during times of economic and social unrest. At these times there is a strong need to pour more money into artistic experience and aesthetic education, not to cut it out from the curriculum almost totally, thus contributing to the perpetuation of social isolation and unrest. In addition there is a need for the opportunity to participate in artistic experience to continue after leaving school. Again, all too often in times of economic hardship, national budgets for the arts are reduced to a minimum with the majority of the finances being channelled into large sacred cows which can serve as national show pieces for the wealthy and elite members of the society (often the same people who have contributed to the paucity of artistic experience and to the general malaise felt in arts education by the majority of the population).

Our experience, as students, scholars, teachers and therapists leads us to believe that the ideas contained in this book are a step in the right direction. The activities we outline all emphasize the sanctity of unique individuals. They acknowledge that each of us is different, requiring different approaches, learning at different speeds and even learning different concepts from exposure to the same experience. We have seen some of these activities used in widely differing settings to achieve the same general results and, conversely, we have seen the same activities used in similar settings to widely differing ends – both as a result of the degree of skill of the leader and the context and purpose of the social interaction in which the activity was employed. We have seen children and adults alike benefit from the use of Social Drama games and from attending sessions over a long period of time.

These activities are part of the Social Drama of life. They are the building bricks by which we have been able to provide a more enjoyable, stimulating and (we would argue) therapeutic environment in which an individual can develop and grow, than the usual one to be encountered in schools and education generally. The activities in this book, and similar ones, have been used to great effect by teachers from a wide range of disciplines – maths, history, biology – to name but a few. It is not that these activities negate the transmission of 'factual' information; rather they place it in an accessible framework, one that enables the learner to recognize their relationship to the rest of his education.

Social Drama does not exist on its own. It owes debts to all other art forms, and is a close cousin of developmental drama, remedial drama, creative drama, theatre training and drama therapy. Like all drama and theatre, it cannot exist isolated from the society in which it takes place because ultimately it only exists by evolving from and reflecting the prevailing social structure of the day. Social Drama complements and is in turn complemented by all the other bodies of knowledge that deal with human development and expression.

None of us will always be able to 'expect the unexpected' but we can develop our skills at recognizing and developing the roles that we and others play. We believe that conventional, contemporary education pays insufficient attention to the development of the basic faculties needed for successful daily interactions and we strongly feel that there is a need to redress this balance. We should return to what education ought to be about: the peaceful and successful sharing of experiences which encourage and enable individuals to learn through interaction. With its emphasis on games, enjoyment and personal attention, Social Drama can help individuals to be more successful in the scenes they act out each day. It can help them to achieve a higher level of personal and social fitness, without labelling anyone as a failure, and so has a major contribution to make to a healthier, more human, individual and therapeutic education.

Finally, as has been intimated so often throughout this book, we feel that education is a life-long process. As long as there is still breath within us there is life and the capacity for learning. Unfortunately, much of our insatiable curiosity is atrophied or destroyed by the experiences we have gained through our formal schooling. One of the greatest joys for us is that Social Drama can be undertaken and enjoyed by people of all ages, from all walks of life and with all manner of formal educational backgrounds. In fact it is the great diversity of participants that has given us so much to reflect on and enjoy over the years. We hope that after reading this work others will be able to share the Social Drama experience with a wider audience than we could ever hope to meet on our own. If only one other person has awakened within them the natural child-like curiosity to enquire about the world around them, then this work will have been worth the effort.

Notes

1 As an introduction to this wide and far-reaching debate, see M. F. D. Young, ed., *Knowledge and Control* (London: Collier–Macmillan, 1971).
2 Dr Sandra Packard, a noted art educator and art therapist, expressed this so brilliantly in her recent keynote address to the Canadian Art Therapy Association at their annual meeting in Victoria, 1982.

SECTION IV

THE MATERIAL OF SOCIAL DRAMA

A. Startlers and Warm-ups.
B. Trust and Sensitivity.
C. Fun and Social Games.
D. Communication Games.
E. Physical Development Games.

The five classifications in this chapter are only a guide, as every game has many uses and many variations. Any one of these games could accurately be placed under more than one heading, but we have tried to give the reader some indication of the ways in which we have commonly used the material. We have given brief notes on the appropriate size of group for each game as well as a list of required materials and preparation. We have outlined some of the potential aims of each game and suggested a few variations (there are actually hundreds for every game). We would like to stress again that there is no 'right way' to play these games. We have described methods and variations that we have found to be successful, but we vehemently encourage you to experiment. Finally we have, where appropriate, indicated a few more important factors that leaders should consider before, during and after each game.

There is room below some of the games for you to make observations or to note your own variations, and some blank pages at the end of the chapter for the new games which you and your group will invent.

We have used the term 'It' to describe anyone who is playing against the rest of the group – often in an attempt to catch or outmanœuvre them. 'It' is often called 'He', 'Her', 'On', or 'On it' in Britain.

At this point we must re-declare our thanks to everyone who has taught us these games, played them with us or helped us to develop them for use in Social Drama. In particular we must thank Bill Morris of Shrewsbury who has helped us with the compilation of this section and who has provided us with descriptions of some of his own favourite games.

We would encourage you to read Chapters 3 and 4 before using these games with your group and to take special note of the advice on preparation and general caution we have outlined. If you are impatient, however, or if you have picked up this book to find material for this afternoon's workshop please go through this 'minimum' checklist:

- Start from where you are, choosing activities which are suitable for your group and which will let you all start from a stable, safe base.
- Read each game thoroughly before using it. Change the rules if you need to and explain everything clearly to the group before they start.
- Make the games fun, for without enjoyment the session will quite probably fail.
- Do everything you think necessary to make the session physically and emotionally safe for everyone.
- Be observant throughout the session, and always expect the unexpected.
- Be ready to adapt any game at any time to suit the needs and abilities of your group.
- Watch and feel for the pace of the session making sure that you 'stretch' your group without moving too far or too fast for people's comfort.
- Always let people opt out of the games if they want to, and never force an issue.

A. Startlers and Warm-ups

1. *Pass the Buck*

Group size:	Any number.
Materials:	A 'buck' – a large soft ball or a cushion.
Preparation:	The group stands in a circle. The leader explains that it is only the person who holds the buck that is allowed to speak. That person, however, will 'pass the buck' to someone else.
The game:	Begin by passing the buck once around the circle. Whoever has the buck says their name clearly. Pass the buck round again, but this time each person says the name of the player *to whom they are giving* the buck. Pass the buck round once more, but this time each person says the name of the person *who has given them* the buck. The buck can now be thrown to anyone in the circle who must say the name of the person who threw it. If they do not know the name they can throw it back to find out.
Aims:	Learning of names; group-formation; concentration.
Variations:	– Add a description of people to their name (e.g. fair-haired Martin; John with a nice blue jumper; Julie with black shoes).
	– Add more personal comments (e.g. Pat, who reminds me of my sister; Paul, who seems a lot more confident than he did last week; Elaine, who was really supportive to me in the last session).
	– Use the buck in discussions. No one is allowed to

speak unless they hold the buck, and if it is passed to you, you must make a contribution or pass it on.

2. Winking Murder

Group size:	Ten or more. With very large numbers divide the players into two groups.
Materials:	None.
Preparation:	The group stands in an exact circle, about an arm's length apart, so that each player can meet the eyes of all people in the circle including people on the immediate right or left. They close their eyes. The leader moves round outside the circle and selects a murderer by touching one person on the shoulder.
The game:	The players open their eyes and look around at the others. They make eye contact with someone and hold this contact for about five seconds, they then select someone else and repeat. They try to meet the eyes of everyone in the group but not in any definite order. The murderer kills people by winking at them. Any murdered player must wait for about five seconds and then drop out of the circle. During the course of the game some of the players will become aware of who the murderer is, either because they have noticed him winking across the circle or because they have a strong hunch. In this case the suspicious player raises his hand and says 'I think I know who the murderer is.' The game continues until another player identifies the murderer. The leader then counts out to three and the two detectives must instantly point at the murderer. If they both point at the same person and that person is actually the murderer, the game ends, and is restarted with

the selection of a new murderer. If the detectives point at two different people, even if one of those selected *is* the murderer, the game continues.

Aims: Eye contact; group formation; introduction to games-playing.

Variations: – The murder victims can die by falling to the floor with a loud scream.

               – When both detectives do not agree on the murderer they have to die.

               – There is one way in which the murderer can always win by polishing off the whole group. We leave you to discover it!

Cautions: – This game is rarely successful with young players, under the age of eight.

3. Danish Murder

Group size:	At least a dozen; better with more.
Materials:	None.
Preparation:	Clear the playing area of obstacles. The players stand in a circle with their eyes closed and the leader selects a murderer by touching one person on the shoulder.
The game:	The murderer *opens her eyes*, the rest of the group *keep their eyes closed* and they slowly begin to move about the room. As one player meets up with another they extend their hands in front. They need to reassure themselves that they have not met up with the murderer. To do this, one player pats the other's hands twice and then waits to see if he gets two pats in reply. They can repeat the patting until they are certain that they are safe. Meanwhile the murderer is moving freely amongst the players selecting a victim. She will receive hand pats from her victim but will give none in return. The victim might try again only to realize that he is murdered. He will retire from the game. The game continues until the whole group is dead. The cards are all stacked in the murderer's favour because there is no way of identifying her during the course of the game.
Aims:	Physical contact without embarrassment; free conversation; group-formation; fun.
Variations:	– The murder victims die with a horrible scream as they fall to the floor.
	– The murderer also operates with eyes closed.
Cautions:	– Take care that people are not stepped upon

during the first variation of the game.
– Some groups deliberately charge round bumping into people.

4. Country House Murder or Murder in the Dark

Group size: Ten or more.

Materials: The detectives might need paper and pencil for note taking.

Preparation: This game is most successful when played in a totally dark room. Failing this the players will have to work for a short time with eyes closed.

The game: Two detectives are selected and sent out of the room. The remaining group gets into a circle and close their eyes while the leader selects a murderer by touching one player on the shoulder. They then move around the room as in Danish Murder. The murderer has his eyes open, selects a victim and commits the murder by putting his hands lightly round the victim's throat. The victim *must* scream whereupon everyone stands stock-still except the murderer. He attempts to move to some other part of the room. The leader asks everyone to open their eyes and calls in the detectives. They move around questioning people who *must* tell the truth. If they have moved after the scream, even slightly, they must say so and explain why. The murderer can lie as much as he likes. After a time the detectives will begin to have suspects. Together they agree on who to challenge. They address the prime suspect with words 'Are you the murderer?' They can only ask this question of three players. If they fail to find the murderer they are sent out of the room to be detectives again in the next round of the game. If they do identify the murderer new detectives are chosen.

Aims: Skill at detection and deduction; observation of body language etc.; fun; group-formation.

Variations: – This game was very popular in large country houses. It is still best played under these conditions (i.e. where the players can move from room to room, and where there is very little light or even darkness). If the game can be played under these conditions all the players come back into a central room after they have heard the scream. All the players except the murderer must still tell the truth but questions and answers become much more complex.

5. Balloon Hockey

Group size:	Ten or more.
Materials:	Several inflated balloons. Two rolled and tied newspapers. Enough chairs for all the players plus two for the goals.
Preparation:	The players are divided into two teams and seated opposite each other with about ten feet in between. Team one is numbered off, then team two is similarly numbered from the other end. The balloon is placed in the centre of the lines, the rolled newspapers are placed about two feet on either side of the balloon. At the ends of the rows the two chairs are placed as goals.
The game:	The leader calls out a number whereupon that son from each side must rush to pick up his newspaper hockey stick and use it to bash the balloon in the direction of the goal. A goal is counted if the balloon goes through the front legs of the chair, the side legs or the back. The players are encouraged to shout their support, often for the other side, and to suggest ways of cheating. They might even join in to help. Nobody really bothers to keep the score. It is rather like 'Alice in Wonderland' where all have won and all should have a prize.
Aims:	Group development; fun; concentration; physical exercise.
Cautions:	– If this game is played too seriously or too competitively it can lead to injury. The greatest danger is of two over-enthusiastic players colliding as they race for the hockey sticks. Warn the group beforehand.

131

6. The Ring on the String

Group size: Six upwards.

Materials: String. A curtain ring or something similar.

Preparations: The group stands in a circle with the string passing through all their hands, which they hold out in front. The ring is threaded onto the string which is tied off neatly. One player, 'It', is put in the centre of the circle with her eyes closed.

The game: The players begin to pass the ring from person to person, concealing it as much as possible. 'It' opens her eyes and tries to find the ring. This is not easy as it is still moving and many people are pretending to have it. 'It' can touch any hand in the circle and that player must open the hand at once. Whoever is found to be holding the ring is the new 'It'.

Variations: – This is a version of a very old game which was almost certainly played in Ancient Greece. The string can be kept in a long straight line with the ends fastened off to solid objects. The players stand along the line with as much as a yard between them. They can run up and down the line which makes it a much more active game. 'It' can work on either side of the line.

Cautions: – As with all games where one person is working against the rest of the group it is important to make sure that 'It' is not victimized. Some people can only take a short spell of the 'It' role and will need to be relieved or to work with a partner.

7. Sheep, Sheep Come Over

Group size: The more the better.

Materials: None.

Preparations: A very large uncluttered space, or somewhere outside. One player stands in the middle; he is the wolf. The other players divide equally at each end of the space.

The game: The game starts with a chant which is repeated after each foray. The Wolf shouts 'Sheep, sheep, come over!' The other players shout in chorus 'We're afraid.' The Wolf asks 'What of?' The players tell him 'The Wolf.' The Wolf then shouts 'The Wolf's gone to Devonshire and won't be back for seven years, so sheep, sheep, come over.' The players at each end then try to cross over and the Wolf catches all he can. All those caught join the Wolf for the next foray.

Aims: Energy control; fun. When adults play this game their faces will light up with sheer joy as they revert back to a genuine child activity.

Variations: – Everybody seems to know the modern variation which is British Bulldogs. The game is the same, only the chanting is missed out.

Cautions: – The dangers in this game are those associated with any team game. There is a danger of falling and of violent collision, but this usually does not happen.

8. Prisoners

Group size:	Any number.
Materials:	None.
Preparations:	Divide the group into two teams. One team are prisoners, the other side are guards.
The game:	The prisoners try to escape from the room. The guards try to contain them. After a while the teams swap over.
Aims:	Physical warm-up; group-formation; fun; ingenuity. The game can also be used as part of your efforts to keep a reluctant and disruptive group in the workshop.
Cautions:	– Add whatever rules you think you need to stop the game becoming violent.

9. One-Line Stands

Group size:	Any number.
Materials:	None.
Preparation:	Split the group into pairs, who are going to have a series of conversations. Each pair labels themselves A and B.
The game:	A is given the opening line of a conversation. B has to reply immediately, then A, then B and so on until a suitable conclusion is reached. (This will take longer for some pairs than others.) There should be no prior discussion about the roles of the speakers or the setting – these should become clear *during* the conversation. When everyone is finished, B is given the next opening line. Some suitable lines might be:

- 'And where do you think you've been till this time of night?'
- 'Excuse me, I wonder if you could help me?'
- 'What do you mean, "You couldn't help it"?'
- 'Look, I don't really know how to tell you this.'
- 'Please.'
- 'I bought this radio here yesterday and it doesn't work.'

Aims:	Introductions; warm-up to role play; communication.
Variations:	– Try, as ever, to fit the material to the needs and capabilities of your group.
	– You can ask some of the couples to show their improvisations afterwards. It is interesting to see the variety of scenes suggested by the same line.
	– Some groups may like to be given more facts

about their characters and the setting before they start.

Cautions: – Be ready to reassure anyone who gets stuck. They may feel inadequate when everyone else is babbling away.

10. *Chair Swap*

Group size:	Six upwards.
Materials:	One chair for everybody in the group except 'It'.
Preparation:	The chairs are drawn into a circle facing inwards. Each player sits in a chair, except 'It' who stands in the centre of the circle.
The game:	The seated players look around the circle trying to make eye contact with someone else. *As soon* as they make contact they *must* change places. As they do so, 'It' tries to sit in one of the empty chairs. Whoever is left without a chair is the new 'It'.
Aims:	Warm-up; group-formation; fun; a good way of mixing up a group who tend to sit in the same place each week.
Variations:	– 'It' can determine who changes places by calling out groups: people with fair hair; people wearing something blue; people who hate school dinners; etc.
	– 'It' can also determine the way people move across the circle: hopping; baby steps; shake hands in the middle; etc.
	– An extra chair is added to the circle. But just before 'It' sits down the person sitting next to the empty chair moves to his right and sits in it. *Immediately* the next person in the circle moves to *his* right ... and so on round the circle. This makes it very hard indeed for 'It' to sit in an empty chair and not on somebody's lap.
	– Try any of these games with the chairs facing outwards.

Cautions: − These games soon become fast and furious and there is some risk of injury. Warn the group beforehand.

                − It is easy to tip a chair over backwards while sitting down. Consider placing the chairs round the edge of the room with their backs to the wall.

                − If the game is getting too fast, introduce a slower way of moving across the circle.

                − This game tends to feed energy *into* a group rather than tiring them out.

11. Yes, Let's

Group size:	Any number.
Materials:	None.
Preparation:	None.
The game:	Any member of the group makes a suggestion, e.g. 'Let's all stand by the window.' The rest of the group summon up all their enthusiasm and shout, 'Yes, let's!' and then move over to the window. Someone else suggests, 'Let's all whistle the National Anthem.' The rest shout, 'Yes, let's!' and do so. The game continues to a natural conclusion.
Aims:	Warm-up; group cohesion; fun.
Variations:	– After a while you can introduce 'No, let's ...' where someone makes an alternative suggestion to each call, e.g. 'Let's all count to ten.' 'No, let's all stand on one leg.' The group divides into two teams according to which of the suggestions they prefer, then the game begins again.
Cautions:	– Be prepared for somebody to say 'Let's all jump on John!' or 'Let's all go outside!' The leader can usually counter these with an immediate call of 'Let's all stand in a circle!' or 'Let's all come back in again!'

12. *Four Walls, a Floor and a Ceiling*

Group size: Any number.

Materials: None.

Preparation: None.

The game: Give your group a certain time (e.g. two minutes) in which *everyone* must touch the four walls
of the room, the floor and the ceiling. Watch how
much or how little they co-operate.

Variations: – Add windows, doors, items of specific colours or
textures to the list.

– Get the group to touch things using their feet,
noses or heads.

Cautions: – Keep the tasks within the physical limitations of
your group to begin with or you may stigmatize
someone who, for example, cannot climb very
high. Later on you can give tasks which you
know will be more of a challenge and which will
require more co-operation if the group is to
succeed.

13. Crumbs and Crusts

Group size: Ten upwards.
Materials: None.
Preparation: Divide the group into two teams who line up, *facing each other* with a gap of about four feet between the two teams. One team is called 'Crumbs' and the other is called 'Crusts'.
The game: The leader calls out 'Crumbs' or 'Crusts'. If she shouts 'Crumbs' then the 'Crumbs' have to race to the safety of the wall *behind* them. If anyone from the 'Crusts' should catch them they must join the 'Crusts' on the other side. If the leader shouts 'Crusts' then the 'Crusts' have to run to the safety of the wall behind *them*. Anyone who is caught joins the 'Crumbs'. The first team to capture everyone from the other side 'wins' – but the leader can easily keep the game going until everyone is exhausted.
Aims: Warm-up; fun; concentration.
Variations: – Move in a particular way; hop; skip; move on all-fours; etc.
               – Keep changing the caller.
Cautions: – It is not unknown for the over-enthusiastic to collide in the middle when a call is made. This can cause injury. Warn the group beforehand.

14. *Contrariness*

Group size:	Seven or eight.
Materials:	An old blanket or sheet.
Preparation:	Seven or eight players sit in a circle on the floor with the blanket or sheet over their feet.
The game:	A leader calls 'hold' or 'let go'. On the instructions 'hold', the players must let go, and on 'let go' they must pull. The leader issues orders quickly and attempts to catch the players napping.
Aims:	Fun; group-formation; concentration.
Variations: –	This is a game of considerable antiquity and has many variations. An energetic variant is 'stand, sit, lie' – on the instruction 'stand' players must sit, on 'sit' they must lie down and on 'lie' they must stand.

15. Tag Games

Group size:	Five or more.
Materials:	None.
Preparation:	Usually none.
The game:	There are many versions of tag. The simplest is 'Tag', 'Tick' or 'Touch' in which one player is designated 'It' and chases other players to tag, tick or touch them. Whoever is successfully tagged takes over as 'It'.
Aims:	Physical warm-up; group-formation; channelling energy; breaking down barriers to play.
Variations:	– 'Off-ground tag' is played as described but players may gain sanctuary by getting off the ground or off the floor.
	– 'Triangle tag' involves mixed groups of three (i.e. two girls and a boy or two boys and a girl). 'It' attempts to tag the odd player in each group while the other two try to provide protection. Members of each triangle must hold hands at all times.
	– For 'Fox and Chickens', the players form a line with Mrs Hen at the front and her chickens holding each other's waists in a line behind her. The Fox or 'It' attempts to tag the player who is last in the line, while the others try to protect him.
	– 'Stick in the Mud' is another tag game which is best played in a confined space. One or more players may be 'It'. They chase the rest of the players and try to 'tag' as many as they can. Players who are caught must stop instantly, stand with feet apart and arms outstretched, and freeze.

They may be released by free players who crawl between their legs. 'It' tries to immobilize the whole group.

– 'Hug Tag' is a superb ice-breaker at the beginning of a games or Social Drama session. 'It' stands at a corner of the games area, calls a number and then pauses for five seconds. The rest of the players must hug together in groups of that number. Anyone not in groups can be chased until tagged. Players should be encouraged to move around amongst each other before 'It' calls each number.

Cautions: – These games can be physically demanding for some people. Do not play them too long.

Youngsters – tend to be *less* rather than *more* tired after these games. They feed energy in rather than taking it out. It is a mistake made by some youth leaders to think they can wear their group out just by having them run around.

B. Trust and Sensitivity

16. *Trust Warm-up*

Group size: Any number able to play a trust game.

Materials: None.

Preparation: Split the group into the pairs or teams that they are about to use for one of the trust exercises in this section.

The game: The members of each set make sure that they know each other's names. The leader then gives them some more information to discover ranging from the superficial to the more personal, e.g.:

- eye colour
- middle name
- favourite meal
- earliest memory
- greatest ambition
- feelings about the session so far.
- When people seem to be working well together, move on to another exercise.

Aims: To break down some of the barriers to effective trust work; to form a simple relationship as a foundation for something more complex.

Variations: – With a group who know each other better the leader can ask them to *guess* this sort of thing about their partner(s), but always give people the opportunity to correct any mistakes.

17. Leading the Blind

Group size: Any number.

Materials: None.

Preparation: All chairs etc. must be moved to the sides of the room, so that there is plenty of uncluttered space. Each player chooses a partner; one closes his eyes to become blind. It is important that the blind people should not peep until the game is over; this will cause a problem for some.

The game: The sighted partner leads the blind one on a walk about, taking care that no harm befalls him. The leading is done by voice and touch. If the exercise is successful the pairs will move about the room with increased confidence and pace. After a while the guide and the blind person are told to swap places and repeat the exercise. Each walk-about should last approximately 2–3 minutes.

Aims: Trust; co-operation at a very personal level; some understanding of the problems of visually handicapped people.

Variations: – The original pairs start the exercise again but the leader fills the walking space with obstacles: chairs, table, balloons etc. This is done silently.

    – Change partners and repeat when the leader silently begins to remove all obstacles.

    – The guide can lead the blind person by touch only; being prepared to speak if there is danger of a collision or of bumping into an object.

    – Lead with spoken directions only or let the group think of other variations.

    – At a later session, especially at a residential course

where a meal is to be taken, let the guides lead their partners to the dining room and feed them.

Cautions: – The safety of all participants is the prime consideration, but because the game is to encourage trust it is unlikely that anyone will come to harm. The leader must keep a special look-out when doing the exercise with young players. Until they have bonded and decided to work seriously they might actually encourage their partner to collide with someone or to bump into a heavy object. This must be discouraged from the outset.

  – We do *not* recommend the use of blindfolds. Sighted people rely heavily on their eyes and will often *need* to look. This is especially true for people who are feeling vulnerable or at risk. It is much better to ask people to keep their eyes closed. In some cases this self-discipline will be quite an achievement.

18. *Surfing*

Group size:	Four or more.
Materials:	None.
Preparation:	Split the group into teams of four or five.
The game:	One player gets down securely and comfortably on his hands and knees. Another player is helped to lay on top of the first, back to back. The rest of the group help him to balance there – one holding on to each arm, possibly another at his head and maybe even someone to help balance his legs. Once balance is established and the player on top is completely relaxed, the kneeling player can move gently from side to side, backwards and forwards and even up and down. The helpers blow gently over the arms, face and body of the surf rider.
Aims:	Trust; relaxation; confidence-building; group-formation; balance.
Variations:	– If members have problems with balance let them lay *across* two, three or more players kneeling side by side.
	– The helpers can hum, whistle or make other gentle sounds throughout the game.
Cautions:	– Be sensitive to the worries of players with a weight problem.
	– Give every assistance to people who find balance difficult.
	– Some people will find this game threatening and will be unable to relax. They can still help other people, though, and will not have to sit out.

19. Grass in the Wind

Group size:	Five or more.
Materials:	None.
Preparation:	Divide the group into teams of five or six, and ask each team to find a space in the room where they can make a small, tight circle.
The game:	One member of each team stands in the centre with the others closely round him. He relaxes and allows the group to push him, gently, in any direction. They push him backwards and forwards and roll him round from person to person. He should try not to move his feet as he is passed around. The group encourages the central figure to relax even more by speaking encouragingly and softly to him.
Aims:	Relaxation, not only for the central figure but also for the group supporting him; trust; physical contact.
Variations:	– The one in the centre closes his eyes.
	– The group can gently lead their charge into a different group.
Cautions:	– Do not allow any fooling around in the supporting circle.
	– Some players will find this game difficult. Let them opt out if they wish, and just be part of the supporting circle.
	– It is important that each player starts gently and builds up to a deeper level of trust. Do not let a team be too demanding in their movements at the start of each person's turn.

20. Exact Balance

Group size: Any number.

Materials: None.

Preparation: Each player finds a partner of about the same height and weight.

The game: Partners face each other with about twelve inches between toe tips. They join hands, lean backwards and try to find a point of balance. (This works best if one player leans back first.) Once balance has been established between them the pair should let their heads lean back and close their eyes.

Aims: Balance; relaxation; trust.

Variations: – As the players become more adept and confident they should work with the toe tips closer together and eventually the toe tips can actually be touching.

– Partners stand back-to-back with arms linked and sag forwards or (at a given signal) they slowly slide down each other to sit on the floor. Some people become so skilled at this that they can sit and stand, keeping their arms linked.

Cautions: – The leader must be watchful and be ready to give assistance if any player is likely to fall.

– In the back-to-back version the group must be especially careful and if the leader sees that any two cannot cope with it he must stop them at once.

– People tend to be 'good sports' and are inclined to do what is asked of them with great enthusiasm, sometimes at some physical risk to themselves. The leader must ensure that this danger never arises.

21. *Same Difference*

Group size:	Six or more.
Materials:	None.
Preparation:	None.
The game:	Someone makes a statement, e.g. 'I like chocolate ice-cream.' Someone else makes a contradictory statement, e.g. 'I hate it.' The rest of the group divide, and gather around the person whose statement they agree with most. Someone else makes a new statement and the game starts again. The statements can be as superficial or as profound as people wish.
Aims:	Simple group dynamics; warm-up to more complicated self-expression; a good game to play before 'Scales' (see game 22).
Cautions:	– As in 'Scales' it can be a good idea to let people opt out of making a choice.

22. *Scales*

Group size:	Any.
Materials:	None.
Preparations:	The leader explains that the length of the room represents a scale upon which people are going to place themselves according to their own perceptions of themselves. Some of the decisions will be harder to make than others. There is also a place where people can 'opt out' of making a statement without fear of stigmatization.
The game:	The leader asks the group, first of all, to stand in order of height, with the tallest person at one end of the scale and the shortest at the other. This is a nice clear example in which the 'rules' of the game can be illustrated. The players then place themselves on a scale in order of their shoe size. Obviously some people will have to move. The next scale could be decided by eye colour: dark at one end and very light at the other. If it is appropriate, the group can now move on to look at more complicated scales: the degree of their individual ambition; level of personal happiness; aggression; left-/right-wing politics; self-confidence; etc. The group will often have suggestions to make, and you can use this exercise to look more closely at issues raised elsewhere in the session.
Aims:	Self-expression; trust; self-awareness; confidence-building; an analytic tool for the leader, the players and the group.
Cautions:	– Any information revealed in this sort of activity

must not be used out of the session without the players' knowledge and consent.

- It is important that players are allowed to go to the 'opting out' area whenever they wish, especially once the self-revelation becomes more challenging.
- It is not always a good idea for the leader to join in the scale, especially when the information is quite personal. It is up to individual leaders to gauge how much they should share of their own personalities.

23. *The Assembly Line*

Group size: Twelve or more.

Materials: None.

Preparation: The players lay on their backs down the centre of the room. The first one has legs pointing to the left and the second one has legs pointing to the right, and so on right down the line. Their heads are touching, side by side. All raise their arms with elbows bent ready to support an overhead weight.

The game: A leader helps one player to lay back on the upraised hands at one end of the line. The player's head is pointing down the line. The prone players then pass the supported player down the line and the leader moves round to support him as he comes off the other end.

Aims: Trust; relaxation; group support; responsibility; physical contact.

Cautions: – No glasses should be worn.

– All sharp objects should be removed from pockets and the exercise should not be attempted until the whole group can work seriously together.

– No one with brittle bones or fragile joints should play this game for fear of being dropped or mishandled.

– People who are worried about their weight may find this game embarrasing. In fact a group who are working together well can support even quite heavy people but, as always, the leader must be prepared to let people opt out.

24. The Wall

Group size: Twelve or more.
Preparation: The room is divided in half by a row of chairs and tables, or better still, rostra blocks. There should be one or two gaps in this wall. Two people are selected as guards and close their eyes. The remainder of the players divide equally on each side of the wall. Each individual has a selected partner on the other side of the wall. The group on one side of the wall is blindfolded, or must keep their eyes closed.
The game: The guards patrol the wall, always being within touching distance of it. One of the sighted group tries to cross the wall without being caught and to rescue her partner by bringing him safely back across the wall. This continues until all are safe or caught. The guards can be changed and the other side has a go at rescuing.
Aims: Trust; careful and stealthy movement; physical ability and agility; listening.
Variations: –   The group always seems able to offer these. One variation is to hold a trial of all those caught after each session.
Cautions: –   The game can be spoilt if players not actually moving interfere by making noises.
            –   Some people hate blindfolds and may need to be able to peep. This does not necessarily spoil the game.

25. Levitation

Group size:	Ten or more.
Materials:	None.
Preparation:	One player lays on her back in the centre of the room. Four or five people stand at each side of her. Another stands at the head and another can stand at the feet. The prone player closes her eyes, rests her hands on her chest and relaxes.
The game:	Working in absolute unison and total silence the team slide their hands gently under the prone player and lift her up. They do this firmly and slowly, and raise her to just above head height. Once up aloft she is swayed very slightly backwards and forwards – no more than two inches each way. Meanwhile, she is being *very slowly* brought back down to the ground. She is then encouraged to relax for a few moments whilst the lifting team moves away. She might then care to say whether the sensation was pleasant or otherwise.
Aims:	Absolute trust and group relaxation; a very definite therapy for both lifters and lifted; physical contact; warmth; group-formation.
Variations:	– A player can lie face downwards and be lifted to waist height only. In this case the lifting team beats a gentle rhythm on the subject before she is lifted and again after she has been returned to the floor.
	– The lifting team can hum or sing gently.
	– By pre-arrangement the lifting team can move slowly up or down the room when they have lifted the subject.

Cautions: – *Never* put pressure on any person to be lifted. Make certain that the group takes the whole exercise seriously; it could be dangerous if even one person is in a mood for fooling about.
– Make sure people lift each other safely. They should bend their legs and keep their backs straight and vertical. If everyone takes their fair share of the weight this should not be too strenuous an exercise.

26. Free Falling

Group size:	Ten or more.
Materials:	One steady chair or small rostrum.
Preparation:	The leader or one volunteer stands on the chair. Ten of the group come close to the chair and by joining hands across make a human mattress. The person who is to fall (backwards or forwards) closes his eyes and counts aloud slowly, from ten to zero. As he calls 'zero' he falls into the arms of the waiting group. The whole exercise is a considerable challenge and several other members of the group are sure to want to try it, and everyone should be offered an opportunity.
Aims:	Trust; group-formation; physical contact; confidence-building.
Variations:	– The wise leader will arrange it so that the first falls are not very far. As confidence grows the human mattress can be made nearer to the floor but it should never mean a drop of over three feet.
Cautions:	– It is important that the catching group realizes that their task is not over until they have put the faller safely on his feet. (I once did this exercise with a sixth-form group; they caught me safely and then thinking that the game was over they dropped me. I had a badly bruised elbow for some days. B.A.)
	– Do not let the group do this exercise if they are in a skittish mood.
	– Even when the faller seems to have an excess of confidence the safety care must be the same.

- Rest the chair against a wall if it is likely to slip on the floor.
- The group should remove belts, spectacles, jewellery etc. before the game.

27. Running into the Wall

Group size: Ten or more.

Materials: None.

Preparation: A large room is essential. All chairs and obstacles must be cleared away. The main group crowds together at one end of the room. They form a human wall, several people deep, but spread out enough to form a good target. They hold their hands out in front of them to act as a gentle 'buffer'. The player who is going to run into the 'wall' stands at the other end of the room.

The game: The runner closes his eyes (this is *essential*) and at a given signal he runs as fast as he can at the 'wall'. Ninety per cent of runners will be quite unable to hit the wall with any force as a sixth sense will check their speed before contact. The other ten per cent might be able to hit the wall at full speed. In this case the people of the wall must be prepared to take the impact safely.

Aims: Trust; confidence-building; group-formation; physical contact.

Cautions: – Glasses and sharp objects are put safely away before the game begins. The game must only be played when the group can be trusted to obey the rules. The group must do this exercise as an experiment in safety factors and for this reason it should only be done with an established group which displays some measure of maturity. It is unwise to let anyone run who is displaying real aggression since such a player will miss the point of the game; he will probably open his eyes and put the catching group at risk.

28. Spot the Difference

Group size:	Six or more.
Materials:	None.
Preparation:	Divide the group into two teams.
The game:	One team turns their back while the other arranges themselves into a simple or complicated 'statue' position. The first team then has a fixed time to study the statue before they turn away again, whereupon *one* person in the statue changes position (it may be no more than a hand or a foot). The first team has to spot the difference. Change over the teams and begin again.
Aims:	Observation; group-awareness; physical contact.
Variations:	– Involve the 'studying' team in setting up the statue. Can they spot a change in something *they* have arranged?
	– The studying team *copy* the statue, but with one significant alteration. Can the statue team spot the difference?

29. I Am Falling

Group size:	Any.
Materials:	None.
Preparation:	Make sure your group know each other's names. Make sure they know how to catch each other safely.
The game:	The group members walk around the room in random directions. At any time someone can call out their own name, whereupon they relax all their muscles. The rest of the group must catch the faller, hold her, reassure her and restore her comfortably to a standing position. The game continues with other people calling their names, falling, being caught and looked after.
Aims:	Trust; group-formation; confidence-building; relaxation.
Variations:	– Fallers can call their name and then count quietly to five before relaxing. This gives the group time to gather round.
	– The leader calls the names instead.
Cautions:	– Do not expect everyone to do the exercise. Some may not feel safe enough and must not be 'forced into trust'.
	– Watch out for rooms full of people called Kate – there may be no one left to do the catching!

30. Sue's Game

Group size:	Ten or more.
Materials:	Writing paper and pencils.
Preparation:	Players sit around the room, each with a pencil and a piece of paper.
The game:	On the paper each player writes 'If I were a colour I would like to be . . .; If I were an animal . . .; a fabric; a flower; a famous person; etc.' and completes each statement. Players may select their own items individually or a master of ceremonies may call out pre-selected headings. The papers are collected together and are read out one by one. Players can guess the identity of each writer. They may call out the names of the writers or, for more interesting results, write down the names of writers and check their lists at the end of the game.
Aims:	Self-expression; sensitivity; trust.
Variations: –	'The Stool of Repentance' – a Victorian parlour game. One player leaves the room while the rest each write down an opinion of him. The player then returns and, drawing the statements from a hat or box, reads them aloud and guesses the name of the writer of each one.

C. Fun and Social Games

31. *The Belly Laugh*

Group size: Twelve or more.

Preparation: The players lay on their backs down the centre of the room in a herring-bone formation, i.e. the first one lays with feet pointing South-West, the next one South-East. The second in the line has his head resting on the diaphragm, or belly button of the first player. All join in this formation so that every head is supported except the first person's.

The game: The first player gives one loud laugh 'Ha!' and it should be such a deep laugh that it jerks the head which is resting upon the diaphragm. The second player then gives two deep laughs, the third gives three, and so on down the line.

Aims: Physical contact; fun; breathing exercise; group-formation.

Variations: – The whole group can be encouraged to roar with spontaneous laughter but this is likely to happen in any case.

– Lay in a circle so that everyone's head is supported.

– Copy the laugh of anyone you can hear.

– Players tell jokes, but the idea is that nobody is allowed to laugh.

32. Happy Families

Group size:	Twelve or more.
Materials:	Prepared cards as follows: Sets of four which include a Mr, Mrs, Master and Miss (e.g. Mr Monkey, Mrs Monkey, Master Monkey and Miss Monkey). There must be a card for each player and all the families should be of different animals. One card is given to each player, face downwards.
The game:	At a given signal the players move around the room exchanging cards. At a further signal the players stop and look at their cards. They must then find the other three members of the family only by making the noise of the animal and/or by miming its movement. When a family has assembled they must find one chair. Mr sits on the chair, Mrs sits on his lap, Master sits on her lap and Miss sits on his lap. The first group to sit in this way is the 'winner'. Cards are exchanged again and the game continues for as long as a dynamic is at work.
Aims:	Group-formation; fun; noise; physical contact.
Variations:	– The game is played with eyes closed and animal calls only.
	– The game is played in silence – very hard to achieve – with animal movements mimed.
	– Other families can be introduced such as Tractors, Teachers, Prime Ministers etc.
	– Use the game to introduce a discussion of sex stereotypes. Introduce non-nuclear families.
Cautions:	– Make sure that the chairs are sturdy.

33. *Grandmother's Footsteps*

Group size: Ten or more.

Materials: None.

Preparation: An uncluttered and rather large space. One player is chosen as Grandmother and goes to one end of the room, where she stands with her back towards the main group. The rest of the group assembles at the other end of the room.

The game: The whole group tries to creep up on Grandmother to touch her. She will swing round from time to time and if she sees anyone moving she points at them whereupon they must return to base and start again. He who catches Grandmother takes her place.

Aims: Fun at a children's game level. Stealth and control of movement. (Children have always realized the values of this game.)

Variations: – Players must move in a particular way (hopping, walking backwards etc.).

      – The group selects one person who they want to be Grandmother next time and try to help him succeed. They can 'sacrifice' themselves or shield him from Grandmother's view until the last minute.

34. Tangles

Group size:	Ten or more.
Materials:	None.
Preparation:	Have a large space cleared of furniture. Ask the group to join hands in a circle.
The game:	Break the circle at one point. Tell the players that no one else must loose hands *under any circumstances*. The leaders are at the place where the circle is broken. One of these leaders begins to weave in and out of the circle. After this is well started the other leader does likewise. They both go under and over arms, constantly crossing the lines, until the whole group is tangled up into a human knot. At a given signal the leaders join hands again. The task is for the whole group to untangle itself without breaking hands. (It might be useful if a few players have been left out of the exercise to give advice to the main group.) The untangling can take some considerable time but it is usually possible to restore the group to the original uncomplicated circle.
Aims:	Fun; physical contact; uninhibited chatter and laughter; problem-solving; group-formation.
Variations: –	This exercise can also be done by getting the group to stand in a huddle, facing inwards. They close their eyes and reach out to grasp other hands, then they open their eyes and, keeping a grip on the hands, untangle themselves. The outcome of this is never certain. It can resolve into one large hand-holding circle, or there might be two or more circles.

Cautions: – Some people will not like such close physical contact.
            – There is sometimes quite strong pulling in the circle. Do not let people tug each other too hard.

35. *The Keeper of the Keys*

Group size: Ten or more.

Materials: A large bunch of keys, or several objects, loosely tied together, which make a noise when moved.

Preparation: One player is blindfolded and sits cross-legged in the middle of the room. At his feet are the keys. The other players surround the Keeper but are some distance away.

The game: One at a time the players creep up to the Keeper and try to steal the keys without being caught. The Keeper cannot move from his position and he tries to catch players by making wide sweeps with his arms. If anyone succeeds in stealing the keys they become the Keeper.

Aims: Fun; stealth; listening; concentration.

Variations: – The thieves are also 'blind'.

            – Once the keys are stolen the thieves have to pass them on as many times as possible without the Keeper hearing where they are.

36. Matthew, Mark, Luke and John

Group size:	Ten or more.
Materials:	A chair for each player.
Preparation:	The chairs are placed in an exact circle and the players seated. Matthew sits at the head of the circle and to his right sits Mark. Next to Mark is Luke and next to him is John. To Matthews's left sits number one and the rest are numbered round from there as far as John.
The game:	All the players continually beat out a quiet rhythm; two light pats on the knee followed by two light claps. Matthew starts the game. *Within the rhythm pattern* he says 'Matthew to – (here he gives any number or an Apostle's name)'. The person whose name or number is given must now take up the lead. He gives his own name or number and passes it on to another. For example, he might say 'Eight to twelve', or 'Eight to John' etc. If anyone makes a mistake or fails to speak before one complete rhythm has been beaten out he has to move to the place of number one and the others move up one place. The players now have to remember that some of their numbers have changed.
Aims:	Concentration; group-formation; fun; rhythm.
Variations: –	There is a fairly complicated variation which is enjoyed after much practice. This is known as the Dropped Stitch version. Suppose Matthew started the game by saying 'Mathew to eight', number eight must pick up the game but will say, '*Matthew* to sixteen.' Number sixteen

follows by saying, '*Eight* to ... (any number or name).' This version is an irritating brain teazer. Some players will think of other variations.

37. Fruit Bowl

Group size: Six or more.

Materials: None.

Preparation: The group sits in a circle with 'It' in the middle.
               Everyone in the outer circle chooses the name of
               a fruit and says it out loud for the others to hear.
               The names must all be different.

The game: 'It' tries to say the name of somebody's chosen
               fruit three times, very quickly (e.g. 'Banana,
               banana, banana'). The player who chose this fruit
               must say 'Banana' (only once) before 'It' has
               finished saying it three times. If the player suc-
               ceeds, 'It' turns to somebody else and tries to beat
               them (e.g. by saying 'Apple, apple, apple'). If 'It'
               does say 'Apple' three times before the appropri-
               ate player can say it once, they change places and
               the retiring 'It' becomes the apple. The new 'It' takes
               over until she beats somebody and inherits the
               name of *their* fruit. After a few goes the game
               becomes very fast – and *very* confusing!

Aims: Fun; group-formation; concentration.

Variations: – Use other sets of objects (animals, flowers,
               famous people).

              – Use people's own names to reinforce an intro-
               ductory name game. (But don't change names
               each time 'It' retires or you'll end up even more
               confused!)

              – Use actions and mimes, sounds or rhythms
               instead of words.

38. Climbing Down the Wall

Group size: Any number.

Materials: None.

Preparation: The group gathers at one end of the room withtheir backs to the wall. The leader explains that the entire room is about to 'tip up' and that they will shortly find themselves 'up in the air'. The floor in front of them will 'become' a wall and they will be at the top of it. The wall they are standing against will 'become' the ceiling and the wall facing them will 'become' the floor.

The game: The task of the group is to climb down the 'new wall' to the 'new floor' without letting anybody 'fall'.

Aims: Group co-operation; imagination; physical contact; fun.

Variations: – Climb 'up walls' or 'across ceilings'.

– Film or videotape the game with a camera tilted through 90° to the horizontal. When you replay it the group really do look as if they are climbing vertically.

– Play other games in the newly orientated room (e.g. play like flies on a wall).

39. Muk

Group size:	Any number.
Materials:	None.
Preparation:	The group sit in a circle with 'It' in the middle.
The game:	The players in the circle sit talking and joking until 'It' says 'Muk!' (the Inuit word for silence). No one is then allowed to make a sound. 'It', however, is allowed to tell jokes, fool around, pull faces or whatever until someone makes a noise and breaks the 'muk'. That person is then given a comic name (traditionally the name of an Arctic animal) and either replaces 'It' or joins him as part of a growing team of animals who will eventually descend on the last, silent member of the outer circle.
Aims:	Fun; exploration of barriers; self-control; group awareness.
Variations:	– Allow 'It' to touch people in the circle.
	– Have an extra rule that if any of the team of animals in the middle laugh at their own jokes they rejoin the silent outer circle.
Cautions:	– A lone 'It' can soon feel very isolated and ostracized. Watch out for this and intervene if necessary. It is often worth having two people in the middle from the outset.
	– Similarly the last person left in the outer ring can feel threatened by a large group in the middle. Consider stopping the game when there are still three or four people in the ring.

40. Cat and Mouse in the Kitchen

Group size:	Two players, an umpire and spectators.
Materials:	A large table (or group of tables). Two blindfolds if necessary.
Preparation:	Put the table in the centre of the room leaving a metre or so of clear space all round. Blindfold a 'cat' and a 'mouse' and set them at opposite ends of the table.
The game:	Using stealth and always keeping one hand on the table, the Cat moves round the table in any direction to catch the Mouse. The Mouse, who must also keep a hand on the table at all times, tries to avoid being caught. When caught the Mouse changes role with the Cat or a new Cat and Mouse are chosen.
Aims:	Fun; sensitivity; listening; stealth; co-ordination.
Variations:	– This is primarily a spectator game. Silence adds a thrill to the game but the calling of conflicting instructions increases spectator involvement. Spectators may take sides to call instructions.
Caution:	– Make sure the table tops do not splinter and beware of sharp corners on the tables.
	– As in other games, remember that some people do not like blindfolds and may need to peep for security.

41. Going on Tour

Group size: Any number.

Materials: Cards, pins or adhesives, pencils and paper.

Preparation: This game requires some advance preparation. Cards should be clearly marked with the names of well-known places around the world or local towns and villages or locations around the house. The first card should be marked 'place A to place B'. The second is marked 'place B to place C', the third 'C to D' and so on. The last card is marked 'place X to place A', so completing a circular tour. Twenty to twenty-five cards are usually adequate for a 15–20 minute game. Before the game the cards should be shuffled and then pinned or stuck in a random sequence around the games area (hall or house, garden or field) in places where they can be seen easily from a metre or two away. However, it must not be possible to see all the cards from one point.

The game: Players may go individually but the game is more effective socially if played in groups of two or three. Each group has a pencil and paper, and, starting at any point in the circuit, collects and records the names of the places in order until returning to its point of departure. The first team to complete the list in the correct order is the 'winner'.

Aims: Social mixing; problem-solving; co-operation; fun.

Variations: – Pictures may be used instead of words or, to make the game more complicated, cryptic clues may be used:

e.g. 1. Birmingham to the capital of France.
    2. Paris to the city with the Statue of Liberty.
    3. New York to ... etc.

42. Squeak, Piggy, Squeak

Group size:	Ten or more.
Materials:	Chairs; a blindfold.
Preparation:	All the players sit in a circle except 'It' who is blindfolded and placed in the centre of the circle.
The game:	The players in the circle change places quickly. 'It' is led or finds his own way to the edge of the circle and sits on someone's knee keeping his arms folded. He then calls 'Squeak, Piggy, Squeak'. The player on whose knee he sits must squeak or make some other sound, trying to disguise her identity. The blindfolded player tries to identify the owner of the knee on which he sits. He is allowed one or two guesses and if he fails to guess the identity he is moved on to another player. A player whose identity is correctly guessed takes over as 'It'.
Aims:	Fun; simple physical and social contact; group-formation.
Cautions:	– This game does not tend to work if the players do not know each other.
	– Some people do not like to be sat upon. 'It' can lay a hand on their shoulder if necessary.

43. *Poor Pussy or Do You Love Me, Honey?*

Group size:	Eight or more.
Materials:	None.
Preparation:	All the players sit in a circle except for the one who is to be Pussy.
The game:	Pussy moves on all-fours and approaches any player in the circle and says 'Meeow'. The player approached must, without hesitation, smiling or laughter, pat Pussy on the head gently and say 'Poor Pussy'. Pussy repeats the procedure two more times. (Three times in all.) If the player hesitates, smiles or laughs he takes over as Pussy. Otherwise Pussy moves on and tries to break the concentration of another player.
Aims:	Fun; group-formation; self-control; introduction to play.
Variations:	– Pussy approaches a player and goes down on bended knee to say 'Do you love me, Honey?' The player replies 'Yes, I love you, Honey, but I may not smile'. This is repeated as before. All sorts of dramatic effects may be used by 'Pussy', but physical attack and molestation are not permitted.
Caution:	– Pussy may feel ostracized or foolish, but this is unusual as the game is almost invariably played in good humour.
	– Make sure the floor is clean and free of splinters.

44. *Shoes for Mrs Doodle*

Group size: Any number.

Materials: None.

Preparation: All the players sit in a semi-circle with the exception of a leader who faces the rest of the group.

The game: The leader calls 'One hammer going for Mrs Doodle'. All the players repeat the words in unison and each strikes his knee with his fist, keeping the 'hammer' going until the next instruction. The number of hammers called into action increases until each player is using six simultaneously: two fists against the knees; one and then two feet stamping the floor; the head bobbing up and down and the tongue moving in and out. The leader then makes sudden changes in the number of hammers called for. Players who are slow to respond may be 'punished', made to pay a forfeit or eliminated. At any mention of *Mr* Doodle all hammers must stop at once.

Aims: Concentration; co-ordination; fun.

Variations: –   This is an old Irish version of the 'Simon Says' type of game and can be adapted in many different ways.

Caution: –   Such complex rhythmic motion (particularly the nodding of the head and the sticking out of the tongue) may be inappropriate or even disorientating for certain groups. Be prepared to use simpler actions where appropriate.

45. *Magnets*

Group Size:	Any number.
Materials:	None.
Preparation:	The group divides into pairs, who then separate.
The game:	Partners run about the room. When they catch sight of their partner they run towards each other only to be instantly repelled. They are 'like poles' of a conventional magnet and no matter how hard they try they can't touch each other.
Aims:	Fun; eye contact; physical fitness; mime skills; co-operation.
Variations:	– Partners become weak electro-magnets: no sooner do they make contact than the current is reversed and they are once again repelled.
Cautions:	– Beware of aggressive magnets!
	– A lot of bodies rushing towards their partners sustaining eye contact throughout can lead to major traffic accidents.

D. Communication Games

46. *Computer Man*

Group size: Two or more.
Materials: Two chairs. A strong drinking mug with a
              handle.
Preparation: Have the chairs facing each other, about four feet
              apart. Ask the players to be seated and place the
              mug, filled with water, in front of one of them.
              Explain that the one who has the mug of water is
              a robot; the other player is the creator of the
              robot. The creator has made the robot in such a
              way that it can simulate most human actions,
              furthermore it is also capable of understanding
              basic human speech.
The game: The object is for the maker to instruct the robot
              how to drink water from a mug. Very exact and
              simple instructions must be given ('Lift your
              right arm.' 'Twist your right wrist towards you.'
              'Swallow!' etc.). If the robot finds the language
              too complex it will not move. If any actions go
              wrong the maker can say 'As you were', when
              the robot will revert to its previous position. One
              of the most important words in the vocabulary of
              the maker is 'Stop!' This game is rather long in
              playing time; it continues until the robot has
              actually sipped the water.
Aims: To get people to co-operate at a very personal
              level and with enjoyment; to learn something
              about the complexity of movement, especially
              those actions which we usually do without

much thought; communication; observation; fun.

Variations: – Although a whole group can gain much by observing two people translate words into actions, the game can be played by all simultaneously. The task can be made more difficult by having the robot blindfolded and the mug of water placed anywhere in the room. In this case there will also be instructions in walking.

– The creator instructs the robot to do other simple tasks – possibly tasks that the group are learning in school lessons or other areas of their life.

Cautions: – Some people are likely to get wet, or at the very least the floor is likely to become so.

47. *Mirrored Building*

Group size:	Two players plus spectators.
Materials:	Two identical sets of children's shaped and coloured building blocks; two chairs and two tables or some space on the floor.
Preparation:	The two players sit back to back, each with a set of building blocks.
The game:	One of the players takes blocks one by one and constructs a pattern or building. While doing this she describes her actions as precisely as possible. The second player listening to the commentary, attempts to build a replica of the pattern or building and must only ask for statements to be repeated when necessary.
Aims:	Communication; spatial awareness; introduction to pair work; co-ordination.
Variations:	– Use more sets of blocks and involve more players.
	– Try telepathic instructions.

48. Origami

Group size:	Any number.
Materials:	A sheet of paper for each player.
Preparation:	Find a player who can make, for example, a paper aeroplane. *Do not* tell the rest of the group what she is going to make. She sits with her back to the rest of the group so that they cannot see what she is making.
The game:	The origami expert makes her paper aeroplane and describes what she is doing step by step. She must not refer to it as an aeroplane or talk about wings or a tail, but can only describe the paper-folding processes. The rest of the group do exactly as she instructs them (preferably without looking at each other's work). When they have finished see whose aeroplane flies furthest. Most of them will look like accidents and will fly about one and a half feet!
Aims:	Communication; listening; co-ordination; fun; problem-solving.
Variations:	– Use other tasks which the group may or may not know well.
	– Have two or more people giving the instructions.
	– Ask some, or all of the players, to keep their eyes shut.
Cautions:	– Some people consider they have 'failed' at this game and will need reassurance.

49. *Quick on the Draw*

Group size:	Eight or more.
Materials:	Paper and coloured pens (large sheets of paper work best).
Preparations:	Draw up a list of nursery rhyme titles (ten should do, but this is often a popular game and the group may ask for more). Split the group into teams of four or more who sit around a sheet of paper and a pen.
The game:	One member from each team stands by the leader and is shown the first nursery rhyme title. They race back to their teams and have to communicate the title *by drawing only*. They are not allowed to talk, write words or mime. The team can ask questions and make guesses until they work out the title. The next player then goes to the leader who reveals the next nursery rhyme title.
Aims:	Communication; co-operation; fun; group-formation; problem-solving.
Variations:	– When the teams have finished they study their drawings and try to identify elements of the 'language' they have developed during the game.
	– Teams can then swap papers and try to unravel each other's drawings. Have the teams developed different languages?
	– Show the papers to people who did not see the game in progress. Can they read the languages?
	– Use proverbs or sayings instead of nursery rhymes. Some are very visual (e.g. 'a different

kettle of fish', 'ladies and gentlemen, I give you the Queen'). Others are much more taxing (e.g. 'Many a mickle makes a muckle', 'Pride goes before a fall').

– Use other things that you are exploring or trying to teach your group (numbers, shapes, letters, etc.) and get the teams to draw these.

50. Chinese Mime

Group size:	Six or more.
Materials:	None.
Preparation:	The group sit in a circle facing outwards, possibly with eyes closed.
The game:	This is a version of Chinese Whispers. The first player goes into the centre of the circle. The second player *only* is allowed to turn round and watches the first perform a short mime. The first player sits down and the second player repeats the mime *as accurately as possible* for the third player. Players must repeat everything they see in the performance (even the mistakes). When they have done the mime they are allowed to watch others performing. The mime usually changes each time it is performed and may be quite unidentifiable by the end. The first player should repeat her original mime once everyone has finished.
Aims:	Communication; observation; mime skills; body language; fun.
Variations:	– Add noises to the mime.
	– Work in pairs.
	– Ask people to change the mime on purpose.
Cautions:	– This game is long in playing and can be frustrating for those waiting in the outer circle. This is particularly true when those watching the performances are laughing riotously. Play the game in reverse order next time around.
	– Limit the time length on the mime according to the concentration span and abilities of the group.

51. *Charade Charades*

Group size: Any number.

Materials: None.

Preparation: The group sit in a circle One (or more) people are chosen as 'It' and leave the room with the leader. The first is given a subject or an object to mime for the rest of the group (e.g. 'elephant', 'spider', 'aeroplane'). Meanwhile, the group is secretly being told what they are going to see. They will make wild guesses at everything but *will not* give the right answer to the charade.

The game: 'It' re-enters the room and performs his mime. The group consistently make their bad guesses and 'It' tries harder and harder. After a while the leader can take 'It' out and give him another charade to try. Alternatively you can tell 'It' the trick and invite in the next unwitting player.

Aims: Mime skills; group-formation; initiation; fun.

Variations: – 'It' is told to perform a totally meaningless mime for the group who are the butt of their own joke.

Caution: – Do not let 'It' get too frustrated before revealing the trick.

52. Who's My Leader?

Group size: Ten or more – the bigger the group, the more effective the game.

Materials: One chair for each player.

Preparation: The group sits in a large circle.

The game: 'It' leaves the room while the rest of the group choose a president. The president then leads the group in a simple series of movements (e.g. rubbing the knee, patting a shoulder, waving the hands, nodding the head, etc.). The rest of the group copy the president's actions but do not necessarily watch him all the time. They may copy movements 'second hand' (i.e. from neighbours). 'It' returns once the game is in progress. Her aim is to work out the identity of the president while the group try to disguise the president's identity.

     After playing a round or two of this game, the speed at which new movements are picked up and the quality of the group's co-ordination can be quite remarkable.

Aims: Co-ordination; observation; group-formation; rhythm; communication.

Variations: – Use sounds instead of movements.
            – Have the group more scattered or even moving around.

53. *Squeeze*

Group size:	Any number.
Materials:	None.
Preparation:	The group sit in a circle and hold hands lightly.
The game:	One player sends a 'message' by squeezing the hand of the person on his right. This second player 'passes' the squeeze to the person on *her* right ... and so on around the circle until the squeeze arrives back at the beginning.

Start with simple messages of one or two squeezes and build up to more complicated communications passing round simultaneously in different directions.

Aims: Physical contact; sensitivity; group-formation; simple communication; fun.

Variations: – 'It' stands in the centre of the circle and tries to spot the squeeze on its journey. If he finds it he changes place with whoever had the message.

– 'It' can choose the sender, the recipient and even the direction the message must travel. This gives 'It' a better chance and means the group must be extremely subtle with their squeezing if they are not to be caught. When the recipient gets the message she says, 'Contact'.

Cautions: – Some groups will not like holding hands.

– Some people will squeeze hard and try to hurt their neighbours.

54. Magic Banana

Group size:	Any number.
Materials:	One or more rolled-up newspapers.
Preparation:	The group sits in a circle.
The game:	The leader explains that the newspaper can turn into anything but this requires the co-operation of the group. They must call out their ideas. A few easy examples will set the tone. The leader 'turns' the paper into a banana which she unpeels and eats. The group will usually guess this one. She gives another example: a cricket bat, perhaps; a guitar; a giant pencil; a toothbrush. She then passes the paper round the circle for everyone to have a go.
Aims:	Communication; mime skills; ingenuity; observation; co-ordination; fun.
Variations:	– Copy the example you have just seen, then add your own version.
	– Add noises to the mime.
	– Give each player a newspaper and have them working in teams (e.g. as an orchestra with different instruments and a conductor with a baton).
Caution:	– Some people find this game genuinely difficult. Let them copy something that has gone before or miss their turn if they wish.

55. *Non-Musical Musical Chairs*

Group size:	Fifteen or more.
Materials:	Chairs.
Preparation:	Half the members of the group (or more depending on the size of the group), sit on chairs placed in a line down the centre of the room. Chairs should face alternately to the left and right of the line. A dummy band (players who mime) is grouped where it can be seen by participants in the game.
The game:	The dummy band mimes under the direction of its conductor. Exaggerated movements are in order. While the band 'plays' (in silence) the participants in the game circle the chairs clockwise. The leader of the game and an assistant remove one or more chairs so that there are more people than chairs. When the band stops 'playing' participants attempt to find a chair in the line and sit down. Those without a chair of their own are eliminated and join the band. The game continues until the process of elimination leaves a 'winner'.
Aims:	Fun; mime skills; co-ordination; observation; concentration.
Variations: –	There are numerous variations to this game which itself is a variation of musical chairs and was devised by students at Shrewsbury School of Art at a party for local deaf children. A popular variant is 'musical knees'. For this the main game continues, but when the band stops playing participants must not only find a chair to sit on

but must also have another player sitting on their knees.

Cautions: – This game does not work unless the rules of elimination are observed. It is a boisterous game. Reserved or 'fragile' members of the group can join the dummy band if they wish.

56. Backboard

Group size:	Eight or more.
Materials:	None.
Preparation:	The group sit in a circle, all facing clockwise.
The game:	This is another version of Chinese Whispers. The leader uses one finger to write a capital letter on the back of the person in front of him. That player writes it on the next back, and so on until the leader receives the letter again. When the group is reasonably proficient at this (there will nearly always be mistakes) they can send round short words, then longer words and (this needs considerable confidence) short sentences. It is interesting to check up on how the letters, words and messages change on their way round.
Aims:	Physical contact; co-operation; communication; sensitivity.
Variations:	– Write the letters on the palm of the hand or the forehead.
	– Send numbers or shapes instead of letters.
Cautions:	– Some people will find this genuinely difficult and may need very simple messages to begin with (e.g. a certain number of pats on the back).
	– Try not to stigmatize people who make mistakes. Point out that they are the ones that make the game interesting.
	– Some people will be worried by close physical contact. Arrange them so that they are less threatened (e.g. sitting beside each other and writing on each other's palm).

57. Mr Shopkeeper

Group size: Twelve or more.

Materials: None.

Preparation: The group sit in a circle. 'It' leaves the room. Those in the circle choose a type of shop and each player chooses the name of something that is sold in that particular shop.

The game: 'It' comes back into the room and stands in the middle of the circle. He says, 'Mister shopkeeper, Mister shopkeeper, what do you sell?' whereupon the rest of the group all shout out their chosen articles *at exactly the same time*. This makes it almost impossible for 'It' to guess what sort of shop he is in. He can ask the question several times and have a number of guesses before he is right or gives in. A new 'It' leaves the room and the group choose a new shop for the next round.

Aims: Communication (or rather lack of it); fun; group-formation; listening.

Variations: – The players can talk, whisper or sing with the same results. It is the amount of simultaneous information and not just the noise which makes the message confusing.

                – Include some 'spoof' rounds (e.g. an empty shop, a betting shop, a Social Drama workshop, etc.).

Cautions: – 'It' may soon feel isolated and need help. Consider having two 'Its'.

                – Don't let the game go on to the point of frustration.

                – This is the sort of game which upsets people in the next room!

58. Word Tennis

Group size:	Any number of pairs.
Materials:	None.
Preparation:	The group spreads about the room. Each pair finds a space and stands facing each other.
The game:	The partners create stories one word at a time, taking turns to add a new word to the sentence. Each word is 'hit' to the other partner across the space between them. The game is played somewhat like a tennis match with the words as invisible balls.
Aims:	Fun; language development; creativity; spontaneity; aid to creative writing and story-telling.
Variations:	– Do not attempt to make 'sense' of the story – the effect is more like 'free-form' poetry than story-telling.
Cautions:	– Try to prevent people 'forcing' their story on their partner (i.e. have only one word in play at a time).
	– Some people do not use their body in hitting the word to their partner and thus become more thoughtful and less spontaneous.

59. *Eye Eye*

Group size:	Any number.
Materials:	None.
Preparation:	Split the group into pairs.
The game:	Pairs take it in turns to give commands to their partner *using only* their eyes. They try to get them to move around the room, sit, stand, pick things up, etc.
Aims:	Communications; pair work; facial gesture; co-operation; fun.
Variations:	– Use one eye only.
	– Add simple gestures.
	– Work in larger groups and develop a dance or movement sequence.
	– Add simple noises. Devise a language.

60. *Visitors' Question Time*

Group size:	Any number.
Materials:	Chairs. A visitor who agrees to take part.
Preparation:	The group invite the visitor(s) to join them in a circle.
The game:	The group take in in turn to ask the visitor a question. The visitor *must* answer with the truth. The safeguard is that the visitor *can* choose not to answer at all but 'turn the tables' and put the same question back to the person who asked it. This person *must* answer their own question.
Aims:	Quick induction of visitors; communication; group-formation; information exchange.
Variations:	– Use this game as a regular part of workshops with members each having a go in the 'hot seat'.
	– Let the visitor(s) ask questions of everybody else but with the same safeguards.
Cautions:	– Some people will feel threatened by self-revelation and will need reassurance.
	– Only use this with a group who are working well and who will not abuse the game, embarrassing themselves or the visitor(s).

E. Physical Development Games

61. *People to People*

Group size: Odd number of five or more.
Materials: None.
Preparation: A person is chosen to be 'It'. The rest of the group is in pairs spread about the room.
The game: 'It' calls commands related to body parts (e.g. 'head to head' or 'knee to elbow'). The pairs then have to carry out 'It's' commands by placing their heads together or their knee to their partner's elbow. Each new command cancels the previous one. When 'It' calls 'people to people' everyone, including 'It', scurries around the room to find a new partner. This should produce a new 'It' who starts the process again. The game continues until everyone has been 'It' or the group tires of playing.
Aims: Fun; body awareness; physical contact; group cohesion; use of imagination.
Variations: – On the call of 'people to people' partners have to shake hands prior to commencing the search for a new partner.
            – 'It' can call two commands at once (e.g. 'head to head *and* knee to knee').
Cautions: – Some people do not like close physical contact.
            – Some people like to shock deliberately. These people when they are 'It' will make calls such as 'chest to chest' or 'crotch to crotch'. This may cause problems for you and the group.
            – There is no one 'right way' of completing

'It's' command. Many pairs come up with extremely inventive ways of doing the same thing.

62. *Trains*

Group size:	Six or more.
Materials:	A clean, uncarpetted splinter-free floor.
Preparation:	Split the group into teams with 3 to 5 in each train. The teams sit on the floor. Each team sits so that individuals face the same way and are close enough to hold on to the hips of the person in front.
The game:	The trains shuffle across the floor on their bottoms to the station (the leader). The first to get there is the 'winner'. If the train falls apart they start again.
Aims:	Fun; co-ordination; physical contact; exercise; channelling energy; co-operation.
Variations:	– Have the train go through an obstacle course.
	– Have a guard (last section of the train) pick up a mail bag (a sweet, pencil or letter) and then get the train to reverse back to its starting point without falling apart.
Cautions:	– Winning should not be the be-all and end-all of the game.
	– Beware of wooden floors, check them for splinters.
	– Some people will not like such close physical contact.
	– Some people will find this very physically demanding, keep the distances travelled short to start with.

63. Boat Race

Group size: Six or more.

Materials: A clean, splinter-free floor.

Preparation: Split the group into teams with 3–8 in each boat.
               The teams sit on the floor as for 'Trains' (see
               game 61).

The game: Each boat crew has to do a certain number of
               'pulls' on their oars. A pull consists of the crew
               all leaning backwards and then sitting up straight
               again. The crew all call out the numbers of their
               pulls as they go. The first crew to do, say, twenty
               pulls is the 'winner'. Any crew who fall apart
               starts again.

Aims: Fun; co-ordination; co-operation; physical con-
               tact; exercise; channelling of energy.

Variations: – Play the game simply for the rhythm and the co-
               ordination and remove the element of competi-
               tion.

            – The boats can move along as they are rowed, but
               it is as good a game if they stay in the same place
               and just 'row against the current'.

Cautions: – Winning should not become too important. In
               fact, if all the crews are shouting out the numbers
               at the same time the result is almost always a draw.

            – Some people will not like such close physical
               contact.

            – This game is physically demanding. Fifteen pulls
               should be more than enough to begin with, and
               some groups may only manage five.

64. *Follow Me Tag*

Group size:	Any number.
Materials:	None.
Preparation:	A person is chosen to be 'It'. The rest of the group spreads about the room.
The game:	'It' decides on the group's method of travel (e.g. walking backwards or crawling on stomachs). Everybody, including 'It', moves in this manner with 'It' attempting to tag someone. When someone is caught they become the new 'It' and select a new way of travelling for the group. This continues until the group tires.
Aims:	Fun; body awareness; physical exercise; channelling of energy; spotlighting; increased range of movement.
Cautions:	– Some movements can be physically very strenuous and care should always be taken to ensure that individuals do not over-tax themselves.
	– Remove any obstacles that are liable to cause injuries to participants.

65. *Points of Contact*

Group size: Eight or more.

Materials: None necessary but music (pre-recorded or live) can help.

Preparation: Split the group into pairs. Explain that you are going to ask them to stand with a certain number of 'points of contact' with the ground. Feet count as one point of contact each, so do elbows, shoulders, backs, heads, etc. Hands count as six points of contact (i.e. five fingers and one palm).

The game: The pairs link arms and move around the room (or dance if you have music) until the leader calls out a number (e.g. 7). The pairs must *stay linked* and must stop with a *total* of seven points of contact with the floor (e.g. one partner may have two feet and one knee on the floor – total so far three – and the other has her back, two elbows and head touching the floor – final total, seven points of contact). When every group has finished they set off round the room again waiting for another call. After a while pairs can combine to form teams of four (still working for a *combined total* of points of contact). Later still they can form teams of eight, and so on until the whole group is working together on one total.

Aims: Movement; body-awareness; spatial-awareness; physical contact; ingenuity; co-operation; fun; group-formation.

Variations: –   The group sing as they play the game, providing their own music until the leader calls the next number.

- People in the group call the numbers.
- Use 'impossible' numbers like 1 and 176 as well as easy ones.

Caution:
- Some people will not like such close physical contact.

66. Breakout

Group size:	Six or more.
Materials:	None.
Preparation:	The group is split into teams of six or seven. Each team forms a tight circle with their arms around each other's shoulders and with 'It' in the centre.
The game:	'It has to break his way out of the circle. He must not kick, punch or use excessive force.
Aims:	Physical contact; channelling of aggression; group-formation; movement.
Variations:	– 'It' has to break into the circle.
	– One person tries to break in while another is trying to break out.
	– 'It' must keep his hands behind his back.
	– 'It' must *persuade* the group to let him in/out.
	– The people in the circle face outwards.
Cautions:	– This is potentially an aggressive game. Introduce whatever rules you think necessary to keep things safe.
	– Remove glasses, watches and sharp objects before playing this and other active games.

67. Back Tag

Group size:	Any number.
Materials:	None.
Preparation:	Split the group into pairs.
The game:	Each pair stands facing each other, about eighteen inches apart. Each player tries to touch their partner as many times as possible in the small of the back, but must avoid being tagged themselves. Neither partner should move their feet.
Aims:	Movement; suppleness; physical contact; fun.
Variations:	– Pairs keep a running score. Anyone who moves their feet loses five points.
	– Try the game with people allowed to move around the room. It suddenly becomes more tactical.
	– Have a 'free for all' with everyone trying to tag everyone else. If people drop out once they have been tagged this game is even more tactical and can last some time.
Caution:	– Such fast stretching and twisting can cause slight injuries and may be too dangerous for some players. Warn people before starting.

68. *Long, Long, Long Jump*

Group size:	Any number.
Materials:	None.
Preparation:	This game needs a *very* long, clear space. Preferably outside.
The game:	The group go to one end of the room or the field. The first player makes a standing-start long jump and stays at her landing spot. The second player now has a run-up of a few feet and jumps from where the first player landed. He, too, stays at his landing spot. The next player now has a longer run-up and jumps from where the second player landed. The game continues until an aggregate long jump is achieved. With a large group this can be *very* long. Everyone's contribution is usually cheered with great enthusiasm and even the poor performer gets acclaim.
Aims:	Co-operative effort; physical exercise; movement; co-ordination; group-formation; fun.
Variations:	– Try the group in a different order to see if they can improve on their distance. They usually can.
	– Everyone jumps backwards or sideways.

69. *High, High, High Jump*

Group size:	Any number.
Materials:	None.
Preparation:	Split the group into teams of three people of roughly the same height.
The game:	One player stands between the other two members of her team and bends her arms forward at the elbow. Each helper puts one hand on the high-jumper's wrist and another under her bent elbow. The jumper crouches, counts to three and jumps vertically as high as she can. The two helpers help her by pushing her skywards but do not let go of her arms. A combined shout at the time of jumping seems to add another few inches to the jump. The others then take their turns as jumpers.
Aims:	Fun (brief elation is perhaps a more accurate term); co-operation; physical exercise; co-ordination.
Cautions:	– Make sure the ceiling is high enough to avoid accidents.
	– Encourage people to land as lightly and safely as possible.
	– Make sure the helpers *help* and don't force the jumper. They should try to make equal contributions to the jump.

70. Fire on the Mountain

Group size:	Twenty-five or more.
Materials:	None.
Preparation:	This game needs plenty of space like a large hall or an open space outdoors. The group forms a large double circle facing inwards in pairs.
The game:	'It' stands in the centre of the circle and calls 'Fire on the mountain, run, run, run'. At this, those in the *outside* circle run round to the right. 'It' then stands behind a partner in the inner circle and calls 'Fire's out'. The runners now and try to find a new partner. The runner who has no partner is the new 'It' and goes to the centre. The inside circle changes place with the outside circle and the game begins again.
Aims:	Physical exercise; fun; movement; group-formation.
Caution:	– This game is physically demanding, especially when played out of doors.

71. *Over and Under, Round and Through*

Group size:	Any number.
Materials:	None.
Preparation:	Split the group into pairs or small teams.
The game:	Each person in turns finds as many ways as possible of moving over, under, round and through a shape formed by their partner(s).
Aims:	Body-awareness; spatial-awareness; physical contact; stretching; suppleness; imagination.

72. Group Carry

Group size: Six or more.
Materials: None.
Preparation: Split the group into teams of six or more. The teams stand at one side of the room.
The game: Each team carries one of its number across the room as safely as possible. The whole team must be involved in the carrying. They then go back carrying another member of the team in a *different* manner. They then cross the room again carrying someone else in *yet another* way. The game continues until the whole group has been carried. This is not a race and teams should be encouraged to watch the variations used by other teams.
Aims: Physical contact; trust; body-awareness; ingenuity; group-formation.
Variations: – Teams make noises as they move across the room.
            – Anyone who sees an interesting idea being used by another team can ask to be carried by that team in that particular way.
Caution: – Being carried is one of the greatest acts of trust. It may be too demanding for some people and they may prefer to be 'moved' rather than carried across the room.

73. *Body Writing*

Group size: Any number.

Materials: None.

Preparation: The group spreads about the room so that each person has their own space.

The game: The leader asks the group to imagine that they are standing in front of a blackboard. She then tells them to take a piece of magic chalk and attach it to a specified part of the body (e.g. the elbow). The leader then asks the group to write on the blackboard using their piece of chalk. To start with writing should be kept simple and specific (e.g. 'write the letter A' or 'write the number 6'). This can progress to sentences in 'joined-up' writing.

Aims: Fun; body-awareness; writing skills; flexibility; movement.

Variations: –   People can work in pairs, taking turns to be a human blackboard.
            –   Use different parts of the body to write with.

74. Monkey Tag

Group size:	Three or more people.
Materials:	None.
Preparation:	A person is chosen to be 'It'. The rest of the group spread out around the room.
The game:	'It' chases other members of the group. If 'It' tags someone that person must drop to the floor and assume a position of a monkey (i.e. knees bent and back of hands on floor). The 'monkey' must retain that pose until they are freed by someone jumping over them. 'It' meanwhile attempts to change everyone into monkeys. The game continues until 'It' succeeds or everyone drops exhausted.
Aims:	Fun; channelling energy; physical exercise; spatial-awareness.
Variations:	– Monkeys can move from a stationary position to get closer to a liberator who must jump over him.
	– More than one 'It' can be used with a large group.
Cautions:	– People with poor spatial-awareness can make mistakes when jumping over crouching monkeys.
	– Beware monkeys who deliberately 'trip' up their 'liberators'.

75. Hunters and Chickens

Group size: Any number.

Materials: None.

Preparation: The group spreads about the room so each person has a space.

                 The game involves two forms of moving. The leader presents group members with first one movement style then the other.

                Chicken: First ask participants to blow their nose and get individuals to force air out through the nose while keeping the mouth shut. At the same time they use their arms like chicken's wings and move across the space.

                Hunter: Ask the group to imagine they are holding stone axes in their hands. Tell them to cleave the air with these axes and to move around the room shouting the word 'who' each time a foot touches the ground.

The game: Once the group have fully explored the two different styles of movement ask them to make a silent choice. On a given command ask them to move either as a hunter or a chicken. Then tell the hunters to chase the chickens. When tagged chickens become hunters and vice versa.

Aims: Fun; breath control; physical exercise; movement.

Variations: – Experiment with rhythms in each movement style (e.g. slow, fast, syncopated, etc.).

Cautions: – Don't allow people to hyperventilate. Keep periods of activity short.

Bibliography

GENERAL

E. Braun, *The Director and the Stage* (London: Methuen, 1982).

M. Esslin, *An Anatomy of Drama* (London: Maurice Temple-Smith, 1976).

J. Grotowski, *Towards a Poor Theatre* (London: Methuen, 1975).

A. Hunt, *Hopes for Great Happenings* (London: Eyre Methuen, 1975).

S. Jennings, *Remedial Drama* (London: Pitman, 1973).

S. Jennings, ed., *Creative Therapy* (London: Pitman, 1975).

L. Pisk, *The Actor and his Body* (London: Harrap, 1975).

P. Slade, *Child Drama* (London: University of London, 1954).

V. Spolin, *Improvisations for the Theatre* (Evanston: North-Western University Press, 1963).

S. Springer and G. Deutsch, *Left Brain, Right Brain* (San Francisco: Freeman, 1981).

B. Warren, ed., *Using the Creative Arts in Therapy* (London: Croom Helm, 1984).

B. Way, *Development Through Drama* (London: Longman, 1969).

CHAPTER 2

E. M. Avedon and B. Sutton-Smith, eds, *The Study of Games* (New York: Robert E. Krieger, 1971).

V. Axaline, *Dibs: In Search of Self* (Harmondsworth: Pelican, 1971).

Eric Berne, *Games People Play* (Harmondsworth: Penguin, 1968).

J. S. Bruner, A. Jolly and K. Sylva, eds, *Play: Its Role in Development and Evolution* (Harmondsworth: Penguin, 1976).

M. J. Ellis, *Why People Play* (Englewood Cliffs, New Jersey: Prentice Hall, 1973).

R. E. Herron and B. Sutton-Smith, *Child's Play* (New York: Wiley, 1971).

S. Millar, *The Psychology of Play* (Harmondsworth: Penguin, 1968).

J. Piaget, *The Child's Perception of the Universe* (London: Paladin, 1973).

J. Piaget, *Play, Dreams and Imitation in Childhood* (Routledge and Kegan Paul, 1951).

J. L. Singer, *The Child's World of Make-Believe* (New York: Academic Press, 1973).

CHAPTER 3

M. Donaldson, *Children's Minds* (Glasgow: Fontana, 1978).

D. Gordon, *Therapeutic Metaphors* (Cupterine, California: Meta, 1978).

J. Hodgson, ed., *The Uses of Drama* (London: Eyre Methuen, 1972).

J. Hodgson and E. Richards, *Improvisation* (London: Eyre Methuen, 1974).

K. McGregor, M. Tate and K. Robinson, *Learning Through Drama* (London: Heinemann, 1977).

CHAPTER 4

P. Barker, *Basic Child Psychiatry* (London: Granada, 1981).

E. E. Bleck and D. A. Nagel, *Physically Handicapped Children* (New York: Grune and Stratton, 1982).

R. Callois, *Man, Play and Games* (London: Thames and Hudson, 1962).

C. DeLoach and B. Greer, *Adjustment to Severe Physical Disability: A Metamorphosis* (New York: McGraw, 1981).

H. Exley, ed., *What It's Like To Be Me* (Watford: Exley, 1981).

D. Ingleby, *Critical Psychology* (Harmondsworth: Penguin, 1981).

I. Lindquist, *Therapy Through Play* (London: Arlington, 1970).

J. Ryan and F. Thomas, *The Politics of Mental Handicap* (Harmondsworth: Penguin, 1981).

R. Shakespeare, *The Psychology of Handicap* (London: Methuen, 1975).

A. Shaw, W. Perks and C. J. Stevens, *Perspectives* (Washington, D.C.: ATA, 1981).

S. Sutherland, *Breakdown* (London: Granada, 1976).

D. Thomas, *The Social Psychology of Childhood Disability* (London: Methuen, 1978).

CHAPTER 5

M. Argyle, *Bodily Communication* (London: Methuen, 1975).

E. Burns, *Theatricality* (London: Longman, 1972).

R. Courtney, *The Dramatic Curriculum* (London: Heinemann, 1981).

E. Goffman, *The Presentation of Self in Everyday Life* (Harmondsworth: Penguin, 1971).

J. Holt, *How Children Fail, How Children Learn,* and *The Underachieving School* (Harmondsworth: Pelican, 1969, 1970, 1971).

S. M. Lyman and M. B. Scott, *The Drama of Social Reality* (New York: Oxford University Press, 1975).

SECTION IV

C. Barker, *Theatre Games* (London: Eyre Methuen, 1977).

H. A. Blatner, *Acting In* (New York: Springer, 1973).

D. Brandes and H. Phillips, *Gamester's Handbook* (London: Hutchinson, 1979).

C. Hoper, U. Kutzleb, A. Stobbe and B. Weber, *Awareness Games* (New York: St. Martin's, 1975).

K. Johnstone, *Impro* (London: Methuen, 1981).

I. and P. Opie, *Children's Games in Street and Playground* (Oxford: Oxford University Press, 1969).

T. Orlick, *The Cooperative Sports and Games Book* (London: Writers and Readers, 1979).

D. Pavey, *Art-Based Games* (London: Methuen, 1979).

P. Priestley *et al.*, *Social Skills and Personal Problem Solving* (London: Tavistock, 1978).

G. Storms, *Handbook of Music Games* (London: Hutchinson,

1981).

M. Torbert, *Follow Me* (Englewood Cliffs, New Jersey: Prentice-Hall, 1980).

B. Warren, *Drama Games for Mentally Handicapped People* (London: Mencap, 1981).

Winners All (London: Pax Christi, 1980).

The Authors

Bert Amies, M.B.E., was County Drama Adviser for Drama and the Arts in Shropshire until his retirement in 1978. He has a long experience of work with all manner of groups and developed his own style of Social Drama in the 1960's. Since his retirement he has been a part-time teacher in 'A'-level drama at a Tertiary College and a freelance lecturer in Social Drama. Bert still lives in Shropshire.

Bernie Warren has over fifteen years' experience in individual and group work with disabled and disadvantaged people. He has worked as a community worker, is a registered drama therapist and was, until recently, lecturing in the Drama Department at the University of Calgary. Bernie lives in Kelowna, British Columbia, Canada, with his wife and family. He is currently working as a peripatetic child-care worker, part-time university lecturer and freelance arts therapy consultant.

Rob Watling has been using Social Drama in community work, theatre training and child-care for ten years. He has a particular interest in the applications of folklore to therapy and has also developed new techniques in the use of video with special populations. He now lives in the South of England where he is co-ordinating a community video project and continuing his freelance drama therapy work.